GLOB

The NEW YORK CITY

MICHAEL LEECH

First edition published in 2006
by New Holland Publishers (UK) Ltd
London • Cape Town • Sydney • Auckland
10 9 8 7 6 5 4 3 2 1

website: www.newhollandpublishers.com

Garfield House, 86 Edgware Road
London W2 2EA
United Kingdom

80 McKenzie Street
Cape Town 8001
South Africa

14 Aquatic Drive
Frenchs Forest, NSW 2086
Australia

218 Lake Road
Northcote, Auckland
New Zealand

Distributed in the USA by
The Globe Pequot Press, Connecticut

ISBN 1 84537 221 2

Publishing Manager (UK): Simon Pooley
Publishing Manager (SA): Thea Grobbelaar
DTP Cartographic Manager: Genené Hart
Editor: Thea Grobbelaar
Cover design: Nicole Bannister
Cartographer: Elmari Kuyler
Picture Researcher: Shavonne Johannes
Proofreader: Alicha van Reenen

Reproduction by Fairstep (Pty) Ltd, Cape Town
Printed and bound by Times Offset (M) Sdn. Bhd., Malaysia.

Photographic Credits:
jonarnold.com/Jon Arnold: pages 22, 72; **jonarnold.com/Walter Bibikow:** page 80; **jonarnold.com/Demetrio Carrasco:** page 45; **jonarnold.com/James Montgomery:** page 23; **jonarnold.com/Doug Pearson:** pages 18, 28, 65, 76; **The Bridgeman Art Library/Frick Collection, New York:** page 25; **Lee Engeler:** page 73; **Thea Grobbelaar:** page 49; **Hutchison Library:** page 78; **Hutchison Library/Jeremy A Horner:** title page, pages 31, 51, 79; **Caroline Jones:** pages 14, 16, 20, 21, 26, 29, 36, 39, 42, 75; **Life File/Andrew Ward:** pages 10, 41, 43; **Lonely Planet Images/Dan Herrick:** pages 7, 27; **Lonely Planet Images/Corey Wise:** page 32; **Larry Luxner:** pages 6, 11, 12, 13, 15, 19, 33, 34, 35, 44, 46, 47, 50, 52, 53, 54, 60, 61, 62, 66, 71, 74, 81, 82, 84; **The Mansell Collection:** pages 8, 9; **Pictures Colour Library:** cover, pages 17, 30, 40, 63, 69, 83; **Alberto Ramella:** page 24; **WPN/Michael Trueblood:** page 70.

Front Cover: *The Art Deco Chrysler Building, pride of Manhattan.*
Title Page: *Street life in the East Village – there's lots of graffiti spraypainted on the walls.*

CONTENTS

MAKE THE MOST OF YOUR GUIDE

Reading these two pages will help you to get the most out of your guide and save you time when using it. Sites discussed in the text are cross-referenced with the cover maps – for example, the reference 'Map A–C3' refers to the Greater New York City map (Map A), column C, row 3. Use the Map Plan below to quickly locate the map you need.

MAP PLAN

Outside Back Cover

Outside Front Cover

Inside Front Cover

Inside Back Cover

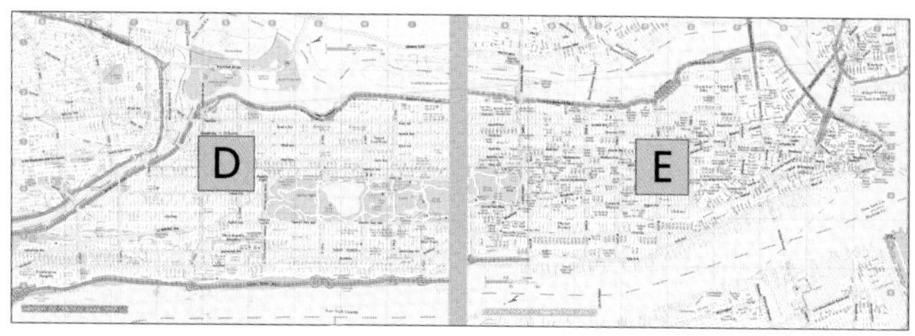

THE BIGGER PICTURE

Key to Map Plan

A – Greater New York City
B – Staten Island
C – Excursions
D – Harlem to Central Park
E – Central Park to Manhattan
F – Manhattan Bus Map
G – Manhattan Subway Map

Key to Symbols

- address
- telephone
- fax
- website
- e-mail address
- opening times
- bus/transport
- entry fee
- restaurants nearby
- **M** – subway

Map Legend

Keep us Current

Travel information is apt to change, which is why we regularly update our guides. We'd be most grateful to receive feedback from you if you've noted something we should include in our updates. If you have any new information, please share it with us by writing to the Publishing Manager, Globetrotter, at the office nearest to you (addresses on the imprint page of this guide). The most significant contribution to each new edition will be rewarded with a free copy of the updated guide.

Above: *The business heart of Manhattan is crowded with skyscrapers.*

NEW YORK CITY

New York is one of those towns that has to be seen by sophisticated travellers. Smart, sharp and sweet, New York is always fascinating. This very exciting city incorporates both the best and liveliest of the American Experience and is always awake. For the dedicated night owl there's no place like Manhattan; equally, for those not intrigued by nightclubs, cabarets or bizarre theatrical events, there is an enormous variety of things to do by day. It's the ultimate urban experience: a place to set the heart and senses racing.

Although not a capital, New York has attracted many to its social melting pot. It's a wonderful mixture, and for the sophisticated New Yorker there is just no place like it.

The Boroughs
New York City is composed of five boroughs but most visitors go no further than mighty Manhattan. You should visit Brooklyn, Queens, even the Bronx, which has a fantastic botanical garden. A ferry ride over the Hudson to Staten Island (actually the fifth borough of Richmond) is a great experience as you take in the Statue of Liberty, welcoming you to her towered city on the waves. Unofficially New York also incorporates chunks of nearby New Jersey, the city's suburbs in New York State (one of the biggest in the union) and what you might call NYC country: the rural stretches of northern New Jersey and Long Island.

The Land

The rivers bordering the east and west of Manhattan are natural dividing lines. The **Hudson River** marks the border of New York City and is also the state line between New Jersey and New York. Even so, these settlements are really suburbs of New York that happen to be in another state.

The **East River**, a short waterway from harbour to sea, essentially an inlet with Long Island as its eastern shore, divides Manhattan from Brooklyn and Queens, while the harbour into which both rivers feed is the division for Staten Island. The East River also forms the channel between Manhattan and the Bronx, becoming the

Harlem River running off the Hudson. Every effort has been made to clean up the Harlem River but it is an ongoing problem.

Plant Life

Some of the city streets are tree-lined, especially in residential areas, and trees and shrubs have benefited from the cleaner air resulting from lead-free gas and catalytic converters. Many residents fill window sills and flat roofs with container plants. It is certainly worth a trip out to Brooklyn in order to see the specialist collections. Or take a trip to the Bronx for the **New York Botanical Garden** with native plants and the **Bronx Zoo**, but plan a day each for these: they are large and the entrances are not close.

Wildlife

Even in the concrete city there is a concern for wildlife. Nest boxes are fixed to office walls for peregrine falcons (they prey on the pigeons, which are pests). Central Park contains rare plants, trees and flowers and in the International Wildlife Conservation Center, you will see some 764 species in their habitats.

Climate

The city essentially has two climates: hot and cold. It's snowy, windy and very cold and frosty in winter, but with a dry, healthy chill that makes for brisk walks and skating in Central Park or in the Rockefeller Center rink. In the sweaty humidity of high summer everyone retreats to air-conditioned offices and apartments if possible. Between these two extremes are brief cool periods of spring and the fall, or autumn, which is frequently characterized with lovely, warm days and clear skies. New York skies are often cloudless and a brilliant blue.

Below: *Camel riding in Bronx Zoo is great fun.*

Manahatta

There is an ancient tale about Manhattan being purchased in 1626 from the Native Indians at a bargain price by Peter Minuit, the Director of the Dutch West Indies Company. The original settlers (then called Red Indians) had infiltrated from Asia across the Bering Sea millennia before, and the Algonquin tribes had spread along the east coast of the new continent. They reportedly received beads and gaudy trinkets worth 60 guilders in exchange for their land rights from the Netherlanders. Whether it is true or not, the original residents called the land 'Manahatta', an Algonquian word probably meaning 'island of the hills'.

History in Brief

Early Settlers

The history of the city begins with the early explorers, who arrived from the 16th century onwards. Little attempt was made to settle until the **Dutch** established a permanent trading post in 1624 which became known as Nieuw (New) Amsterdam.

The Dutch stayed for half a century but New Amsterdam wasn't destined to last as a Dutch settlement. **Britain** was eager to increase her overseas possessions, and in 1664 Charles II gave the colony to his brother, the Duke of York. British warships blockaded New York harbour and took the city without firing a single shot. New Amsterdam was then renamed New York.

New York prospered under British rule and by the mid-18th century had become a major port. On the eve of the Revolution it was the second largest city in the colonies with 20,000 citizens. It was also strategically vital during the **War of Independence** (1776–83). But the colonies eventually won their freedom and the British were forced to concede control of the city.

Although it had kept a low wartime profile, New York was briefly the new nation's capital (1785–90) to be followed by Philadelphia (1790-1800). In 1789 **George Washington** was inaugurated as President of the United States in New York's new Federal Hall. Around this time the city developed an infant financial infrastructure by opening the first bank and a stock exchange, thus laying the foundations for its role as a world financial centre.

Below: *This contemporary etching depicts the tough, arrogant man who was Peter Stuyvesant.*

Despite the British blockade of New York harbour in the War of 1812, the city continued to prosper. By the middle of the century, New York was the most prosperous city in the country; traders and industrial tycoons were making fortunes. Manufacturing increased and the rich moved uptown.

Above: *The nation's first president, George Washington.*

Immigration

In the 19th century immigration rolled in like a tide, and New York was the main receiving point for European settlers. Africans were brought in to the southern ports of the USA as slaves. Many moved north to find a free life and in New York they headed for the borough of Harlem.

From 1840–57, three million **Irish** and **Germans** arrived in New York harbour. Most fanned out across America to create a new nation, though many stayed in the city. New York was unprepared for such an influx: fires, epidemics, overcrowding and fearful poverty ensued, and there were riots and looting.

From 1870 a new wave of **Italian, east European** and **Chinese** immigrants arrived. Ellis Island opened in 1892 to facilitate their entry. At the turn of the century, the population density of the Lower East Side (where most of the immigrants lived) was 330,000 per sq mile, the highest in the world. Living and working conditions were appalling and didn't improve until after the Triangle Shirtwaist Factory fire in 1911, when 146 young women working in a sweatshop were burned to death. Tougher laws and fire escapes were then implemented.

The Making of the Metropolis

As Manhattan flowed relentlessly north, hemmed in by its two rivers, it developed a series of defined districts. Inevitably many of these have changed, some beyond all recognition – for this was originally an island of small farms. It may be hard to imagine now, especially as these rural settlements have become the Financial District. The Lower East Side is no longer the same place where waves of 19th-century immigrants settled in overcrowded tenement buildings, and Midtown retains few of its original distinctive brownstone row houses.

Above: *The Immigration Halls on Ellis Island, where new arrivals were processed for a century, now houses a museum.*

Prohibition
As alcohol was denied under legislation in 1919, so illegal drinking of 'bathtub gin' and other home-made liquors grew and crime prospered in the new lucrative market. Speakeasies (drinking dens) flourished all over New York. It was fashionable for the wealthy to go up to Harlem to the Cotton Club to dance, drink and drug, to hear the new jazz and see the black stars emerging from that vital hotspot. The way that most poor Harlem residents lived was totally unknown to most well-off New Yorkers, but it was smart and life was fast and exhilarating.

Between the Wars

The 1920s were a time of growth and high living, epitomized by New York's flamboyant mayor, Jimmy Walker. Alcohol was outlawed but speakeasies flourished. The economic boom began to spiral out of control and confidence in the stock market came to an abrupt end with the **Wall Street Crash** in October 1929. By 1932 Walker had resigned amid accusations of corruption. More than a quarter of New Yorkers were out of work and thousands lived in shantytowns. The USA was in the grip of the terrible **Great Depression**. This continued until the mid-1930s. In New York the WPA (Works Progress Administration) was greatly responsible for the city's economic recovery, creating thousands of jobs and encouraging projects from construction to artworks.

Post-War New York

After 1945 the accent was on growth. The United Nations established its headquarters here in 1946, and Idlewild Airport (renamed John F. Kennedy Airport after the president's assasination in 1963) was opened in 1948 to encourage more business. The flood of immigrants had slowed down so much that in 1954 Ellis Island processed its last New American.

The city almost went bankrupt in the 1970s but experienced an economic boom in the 1980s, a crash in '87, then growth from the early '90s. Much of NYC has been regenerated, but there remains a marked polarity between rich and poor.

Government and Economy

The mayor of New York is no mere figurehead: he (or maybe one day she) is a very powerful political force, as epitomized by Mayor Fiorello LaGuardia or, more recently, Rudolph Giuliani. The current mayor of New York is Michael R. Bloomberg.

In 1989 New York's government was reformed and now it is a 35-member city council. Each of the five boroughs has a certain amount of independence of legislation.

Economic Development

New York is first in so many fields. The number one city in the United States, it is also the biggest conference and incentive meeting place in the country. It's the major business and financial centre, with the number one stock exchanges. Although trade by sea has fallen away, it still acts as a major port and its three airports handle cargoes from around the world. Industry is a giant and there's constant encouraging of new companies to come and set up. Fashion and the garment industry are big employers. Tourism is a major money-winner, bringing billions to the city each year, making it the most exciting visitor destination in the world. The theatre and entertainment industries, volatile though they are, flourish and encourage the growth of other industries, from taxi services and parking lots to hotels and restaurants. The arts are big money here – major auction houses flourish and there is more book publishing than anywhere else in the country.

The Wall Street Crash

Although there had been warnings and tremors, the Crash was not expected and everyone was encouraged to gamble. Huge sums were being made on the Stock Market and this paved the way for a dreadful and shocking fall in October 1929 that paralyzed not only the United States but the whole world. It resulted in the Depression and New Yorkers suffered as much as the rest of the country. Strangely enough, there was some growth during this period – such as civil projects which included the construction of the city's skyscrapers and Rockefeller Center.

Below: *National Debt Clock.*

Postal Codes
If you have been given an address in Manhattan you may not have much idea where it is, even though cross streets are consecutively numbered. Avenues are long and there are some named (not numbered) roads, for example, Columbus, Amsterdam, Greenwich and Park Avenue, Central Park South and West. The postcode system is simple: addresses in Manhattan have a set of five numbers, and the last two digits tell the district. Post office maps show the areas; for example 10036 is Midtown and Theater District; 10011 Greenwich Village–Lower Fifth Avenue; and 10028 is Upper East Side.

The People

New York City has flattened out in terms of population growth and, like London, now maintains a figure of above 7 million. These two cities, having long claimed to be the biggest in the world, are now far smaller than São Paulo in Brazil and Mexico City. Yet New York has always been diverse, always received the mass of new citizens, and it remains a mixture of many races. This will be evident on your first subway trip!

Over half of the population is white, about one-quarter is black, and there is a large sprinkling of Asians as well as Native Americans. There's really no ethnic majority, but a number of minorities. Hispanics are now the most numerous in this grouping.

Of the original European settler groups, many still live in New York and, while not as numerous as they once were, the Irish, Italian and Jewish citizens do still make a vital and concerned contribution to city life and government. This is sometimes evident in specific areas: at one time half of the New York police force seemed to be Irish. More recent arrivals have been from the Caribbean (especially Puerto Rico and Haiti) and a considerable influx has also been received from Russia, India, Central America and Southeast Asia. New arrivals tend to group together. For example, you'll find many fruit and vegetable stands run by Vietnamese and Korean people on the Lower East Side.

Below: *Oriental carpets for sale in one of the city's many markets.*

Language

Above: *People walking on 5th Avenue, New York's premier shopping area.*

Although to all intents English is the first language, Americans sometimes use different words to mean different things. You will find an example of these Americanisms on page 88. Although you will have no difficulty in being understood in New York, Spanish has unmistakably made its mark and is a growing language. Signs on shops, boardings, subways and buses are catering more and more for Hispanics. Spanish-speaking citizens, who are mostly from Puerto Rico, Cuba and South and Central America, have brought a new mixture and lively presence to this ever-changing city.

Apart from these two languages, there are many others to be heard as you walk around the principal streets. Yiddish was once prevalent, although less frequently heard now. Italian, Russian, Turkish and Greek have their own areas, and in Chinatown you can hear not one but several of the Chinese dialects.

Religion

Religions run the gamut of world beliefs, alongside all kinds of cults. Although long ago the established religion was essentially Protestant in its many forms, Catholicism is a big force, established by the immigrants from Ireland and Italy. New York's two most famous churches are St John the Divine and St Patrick's. There are many synagogues, mosques and temples. Whatever your belief, you will find some element of it in this city.

New York Humour

Like all great cities, from London to Berlin and Paris to Sydney, New York has its own decided sense of humour. It probably started with the immigrants, who had to be cheerful to keep going. New York certainly has roots with Jewish comedians of Yiddish theatres of the Lower East Side, and the city continues to take in new forms as new residents arrive. This type of humour continues to inspire many New Yorkers, especially in today's tough times.

Empire State Building
350 5th Ave at 34th St, 101118
212 736 3100
info@esbnyc.com
www.esbnyc.com
09:30–00:00 daily
5th Avenue and 34th Street
M West 34th Street
There are places to eat outside and inside. There's also a gift shop.

See Map E–C4 ★★★

EMPIRE STATE BUILDING

This elegant building which still towers over 34th Street, contrasting with clusters of high buildings in Lower and Midtown, is a gem of Art Deco constructed during the Depression. Famous as a landmark from the day it was completed, its steel frame enables it to stand at 1454ft (443m). It is often floodlit in colour and looks marvellous at sunset, sometimes with its head in the clouds, when light glints on its windows and metallic fittings.

You can ascend the tower to the observation platforms. Note the lavish Art Deco foyers and elevator banks before ascending to the platform on the 86th floor. From the observatory here you gain great views of the city, and a trip up by express elevator is still one of the top Manhattan treats. Try a late night visit. Allow plenty of time for a visit as it's very popular, especially on weekends and public holidays. Preferably go either early or late, otherwise it can be very crowded and you will waste time standing in numerous lines. However, it means you may get a chance to chat to other visitors from all over the USA and the world too. Take photo ID.

Although not so high, the central tower of **Rockefeller Center** (*see* page 18) further uptown on Fifth Avenue now allows visitors, so it's a possible alternative.

Below: *You can't avoid seeing some of New York's famous buildings, and the Empire State makes for a special photograph.*

See Map A–A3 | ★★★

STATUE OF LIBERTY

Above: *A glorious gift to the USA from France in the 1870s, the Statue of Liberty is spectacular.*

A gift from the French, Liberty, a magnificent work by French sculptor Frédéric Bartholdi, and now the symbol of New York City, almost didn't make the journey. She very nearly foundered at sea, and on arrival had to wait in huge chunks to be assembled, and then for money to be raised by donations before being set atop her pedestal in 1886.

The statue is 305ft (93m) high from the ground to the tip of the torch and offers magnificent views from its crown and observation deck (currently closed, but check). It's advisable to get there early (free ferry from the Battery) and you take an elevator up once inside. However, with the country's fears about security it's unlikely you will be able to ascend into the crown. There are ongoing discussions over accessibility and you may only be able to get mid-way, which rather spoils the whole idea of a visit, especially if it results in a string of viewing portholes around Liberty's tummy!

There were fears for the statue's safety after 9/11 but, as it's often pointed out, if 'Lady Liberty' ever is struck down, the French apparently still have the original 19th-century sculptor's moulds!

Statue of Liberty
✉ Liberty Island, NYC 10004
☎ 212 363 3200
💻 www.statueoflibertyferry.com
🕒 09:30–17:00 daily
🚌 M1, M6, M9, M15
M Battery

See Map E–C4 ★★★

TIMES SQUARE AND BROADWAY

Below: *Times Square isn't a square, it's a confluence of roads.*

Times Square is still crowded and lit up with advertising signs but has nevertheless retained some kind of glamour. The square is actually a triangle extending from 42nd to 45th Street, the point at which Seventh Avenue crosses Broadway. There are many restaurants, bars and shops, and best of all are the nearby **theatres of Broadway** which are a big lure to many of the city's visitors. Look for the half-price booth called TKTS at the top of the square for bargains (*see* panel, this page).

There are tourist information booths and a handy official one at the old Embassy Theater lobby on Broadway, open every day. The ***New York Times***, the daily newspaper that gave the square its name, occupies a somewhat grim set of buildings on West 43rd Street. For many, Times Square is quite simply the centre of town.

Over the past few years the area has been cleaned up and dramatically transformed: even 'Hell's Kitchen' in the West 40s has upgraded. Large new hotels and new theatre developments (including old ones reopened) have helped make this area safe, and once-dilapidated West 42nd Street beyond 7th Avenue has been vastly improved.

Cheap Seats

On Times Square is a popular booth called TKTS where people queue every day for cheap tickets to shows. It offers off- and on-Broadway matinees and evening shows, on the day of the performance only, usually at half-price plus a small fee. Daily allocation of seats can be small, so some sell out. Shows offered are indicated on notice boards, and can include some hits.
✉ Times Sq, 47th St
☎ info: 212 221 0885
☎ listings: 212 768 1818, 💻 www.tdf.org

See Map B–C1 | ★★★

STATEN ISLAND FERRY

Your journeys of discovery round New York don't have to be exclusively on the road or the underground. You can go by boat and in any case you can only get to Staten Island from Manhattan by ferry. And what a trip! If the weather is fine you can spend half a day or more on Staten Island and take the ferry from the Battery in Lower Manhattan. The journey across the harbour adds considerably to the fun.

Staten Island is a part of Richmond, a surprisingly large borough offering views of **Lower Manhattan, Ellis Island** (*see* page 29) and the **Statue of Liberty** (*see* page 15) and an introduction to the city's busy harbour as well. Here you can find several interesting things to see, including **Historic Richmond Town** (a restored example of an early New York village), the historic **Snug Harbour Cultural Center** and the **Jacques Marchais Center of Tibetan Art**.

It's a pity more people don't explore this option, since the Staten Island Ferry is free for foot passengers. You get a marvellous sightseeing voyage, and when crossing the harbour, you can see maritime traffic crowding the water. You disembark from the ferry on tranquil Staten Island, and can look back at the grand spectacle of Manhattan rising magnificently from the waves.

Cruising Around the City

Aside from the famous ferry, you can take several cruises. New York is a city on the water and outings depart from several points. **Shark** is a 30-minute speedboat ride. **Circle Line Cruises** depart from berths at Pier 83, West 42nd Street. If you would like a more formal trip with dinner, the **World Yacht** leaves from Pier 81 and gives a lunch, brunch or dinner excursion. From Lower Manhattan's Pier 16 you can cruise the harbour on **Seaport Liberty Cruises**, sailing regularly from South Street Seaport in Lower Manhattan; most will have live music. For more cruising options, *see* panel, page 47.

Below: *The old Staten Island ferries, serving commuters, make a great free ride for tourists too.*

Rockefeller Center
5th Ave, between 48th and 51st streets
212 632 3975
tours: 212 664 3700
rink: 212 332 7655
www.rockefellercenter.com
M trains B, D, E, F, V
M1, M2, M3, M4, M5, M6, M7, M27, M50, Q32

Radio City Music Hall
6th Ave at 50th St., NYC 10020
212 247 4777
www.radiocity.com
M trains B D F V
M5, M6, M7, M27, M50

See Map E–B4	★★★

ROCKEFELLER CENTER

Between 47th and 52nd Streets off Fifth Avenue, this centre is one of New York's great pieces of urban planning. It has a set of stylish 1930s buildings, gardens and walks set in 11.7ha (29 acres) at the heart of Midtown, opposite St Patrick's Cathedral (*see* page 21). Walk down the main avenue with its glorious flowery gardens to the central sunken plaza – a great place for New York socializing! The plaza is an open-air restaurant in summer and in winter it becomes a skating rink under the statue of Prometheus. There are lots of stylish shops and do take note of the individual detailing of this rich monument to Art Deco in metalwork, tiles, glass and sculptures.

At the rear of the Rockefeller Center, within the complex itself, is a mammoth theatre that is a New York institution: **Radio City Music Hall**. It was opened in December 1932 after having been lovingly restored. With almost 6000 seats, this is America's showplace, especially when the big Christmas Spectacular has the legendary Rockettes high-kicking. In high Art Deco style, it has fabulous decors – even the men's toilet is in the period! If you can't see a show, take an hour-long tour for a modest fee. They give you an introduction to both front and backstage aspects of a great American theatre.

Below: *During the year there are always crowds at Rockefeller Center, and in winter there's ice skating.*

See Map E–B4 | ★★★

MUSEUM OF MODERN ART

Above: *The redesigned Museum of Modern Art, with a host of treasures, always has a stream of visitors.*

The great collection has become an art object itself: walk around new rooms, vast galleries, airy spaces, with a sense of bringing New York itself into the redeveloped building. It's a really novel experience, with new viewpoints everywhere affording the chance to see works and rooms from many angles. Everywhere wide windows show chunks of nearby streetscapes and reflected façades. Newly returned from a base in Queens, modern MoMA has been turned inside out – it's now very theatrical and it's really fascinating.

Often considered to be *the* temple of modern art, for many the museum is one of the greatest shows this amazing city can offer. All the great American artists are here, as well as famed European works from Chagall and Picasso to Mondrian, and the ground floor garden with its flower beds and pools has star sculptures.

However, MoMA embraces as its special preserve all the modern arts from films to photography, painting to prints, bibelots to books, as well as architecture and new design. There are study facilities too.

Since it first opened in 1929, MoMA has been both pleasing and shocking and it often makes news. More popular than ever now it has returned to West 54th Street and Fifth Avenue, it is likely to be so popular you may need to purchase tickets in advance. If new and vital contemporary arts are your pleasure, don't miss it.

Museum of Modern Art
✉ 11 West 53rd Street, NYC 10019
☎ 212 708 9400
www.moma.org
Wed–Mon 09:30–17:30
Tickets are $20, + concessions; Fri free 16:00–20:00
M1, M2, M3, M4, M5, M6, M7, M50, M57

Above: *Brooklyn Bridge, a New York landmark.*

See Map E–H2 ★★★

SOUTH STREET SEAPORT AND BROOKLYN BRIDGE

Allow a lot of time to see the evocative **South Street Seaport**, a large place with several aspects. A long-term project to mark the city's vital maritime history (it was founded because of the fine harbour), this 11-square block project commemorates a time when New York was sovereign of the sea. Goods arrived from around the world and from the birth of the new country, trade increased with a fierce vitality.

In its great days South Street was a forest of masts and tackle, an image this very good 'living' museum attempts to perpetuate. Aside from visiting the seven sailing ships moored here, all meticulously restored, you can actually sail on one, the *Pioneer*, a schooner dating from 1885, or take harbour cruises on the replicas of old craft in the evening for music and drinks. Circle Line and Seaport Liberty ships (*see* panel, page 17) go from Pier 16 and offer a 60-minute narrated trip. Jazz concerts are held at the Seaport in summer.

A handsome arch over the East River, and a New York legend, the **Brooklyn Bridge** is a 19th-century marvel created by John Augustus Roebling. With a span of almost 1600ft (488m), it opened in 1883 and took 14 years to build. It's a major artery feeding into Lower Manhattan, and also a grandstand for pedestrians to view the river craft and the skyline from elevated footways.

South Street Seaport
✉ East River at Fulton Street
☎ 212 732 7678
🖳 www.southstreetseaport.com
M trains 2, 3, 4, 5, A, C, J, M, Z
🚌 M9, M15

See Map E–B3 ★★★

ST PATRICK'S CATHEDRAL

A magnificent twin-spired 19th-century Gothic construction, St Patrick's Cathedral is the seat of the cardinal of New York and America's biggest Catholic cathedral. Situated at the centre point of Fifth Avenue, the Cathedral is the the focus of the annual St Patrick's Day Parade. It's very much a centre of worship, its cool interior flickering with candles.

Although it originally stood tall on its famous thoroughfare, this large church in approved ecclesiastical style is now somewhat dwarfed by nearby midtown buildings. Once you are close to it, however, the presence is still impressive, with a flight of stone steps leading down to Fifth Avenue. Constructed rapidly, for an ornate Gothic-style cathedral, between 1858 to 1879, it was built to replace a much smaller outgrown downtown structure. (Originating in the lower Manhattan Italian section, it still exists within what is now Chinatown.) One of the richest and most powerful of archdioceses, it has had colourful prelates – notably the worldly Cardinal Spellman who supposedly blessed the Vietnam War. To hear such stories, however, you will have to ask knowing New Yorkers.

The elegant interior, with its fine stained-glass windows, makes this atmospheric building a very popular free attraction.

St Patrick's Cathedral
⊠ 5th Avenue and East 51st Street, NYC 10022
☎ 212 753 2261
www.archdiocese.org
M1, M2, M3, M4, M5, M27, M50, Q32
M trains 6, E, V

Below: *Tall, pointed Gothic arches, magnificent rose windows and sculptured columns make the interior of St Patrick's impressive.*

Centre Point
The business and shopping hub of the Village is where Eighth Street runs into Sixth Avenue. Here a major subway stop (West Fourth Street station) unloads visitors and locals alike, and there are lots of news, flower and hot-dog stands. The Village is excellent for good food shops: many small specialist ones and groceries spill out onto the sidewalks and liquor stores rub doorways with smart shops and galleries. Looming above busy Greenwich Avenue and 10th Street is the clock tower of the Jefferson Market Courthouse. In the evening the place is even livelier.

See Map E–F3/4 ★★★

GREENWICH VILLAGE AND WASHINGTON SQUARE

'The Village', as it is known, is an easy-going area with a relaxed attitude. Though basically a smart residential area, Greenwich Village still has a focus on creativity, and it can still trot out a few rather hardy eccentrics. If you wander up and down Eighth Street, the Avenue of the Americas (still known here as Sixth Avenue) and along such streets as Christopher, Bleecker, Charles, Grove and Waverly Place, you will get a feel for this fascinating quarter.

Washington Square, set to one side of the Village, is a vibrant space – quintessential New York. The stone arch, completed in 1895, honours George Washington. The square marks the beginning of Fifth Avenue and has been mentioned in literature. No. 16 is famed for being the setting for Henry James's novel *Washington Square*.

At Astor Place (with a notable subway station) there's a junk market and a modern sculpture of a big black cube. This is supposed to be movable so passers-by can interact and have a game with it.

Romanesque-style Judson Memorial Church, on the south side, is part of New York University, which clusters to the east of Washington Square. NYU students use the square as an impromptu campus, and figures hunch for what seems like an eternity over chess and board games. This is a good place to stroll and observe people.

Below: *Washington Square, with its stone arch commemorating George Washington.*

See Map D–H4 | ★★★

METROPOLITAN MUSEUM OF ART

Above: *The Metropolitan Museum of Art on Fifth Avenue.*

This is one of the greatest repositories of art in the world. This palatial building should not be missed, whether you are fond of art or not. It's a showplace and a bit awe-inspiring; as you ascend the grand steps you have a real sense of occasion.

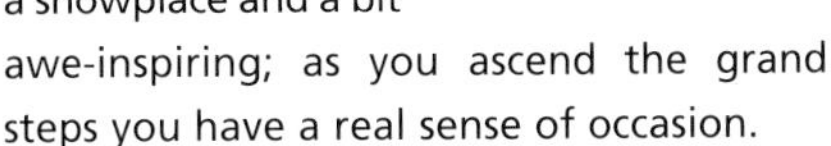

Like the Louvre or the British Museum, this is a star collection of major items, and you can only hope to see a part of it in a day's visit. It's absolutely huge: its many rooms encompass not just a great number of pictures but also sculpture, decorative arts and furniture, arms and armour, costume, and a whole range of antiquities. In addition there are regular exhibitions, some of them major retrospectives of particular artists or movements.

The American Wing is fabled, there are whole buildings from Ancient Egypt, an Assyrian lion, and rare and remarkable Vermeers. Van Gogh's *Irises* and *Cypresses* are here, too. Guided tours are available on request. There's a restaurant where you can snack or have a meal. Entry is by voluntary donations and you may give what you can afford, but it would be appreciated if you pay the full suggested amount, as this helps to cover the cost of special exhibitions, for which there is no additional charge or special ticketing.

Metropolitan Museum of Art
✉ Fifth Avenue at 82nd Street, NYC 10028
☎ 212 535 7710
🖳 www.metmuseum.org
🕒 09:30–17:30 Tue–Thu and Sun, 09:30–21:00 Fri–Sat
💰 voluntary donations
🚌 M1, M2, M3 M4, M79, M86
M trains: 4, 5, 6

See Map E–A4 ★★★

CENTRAL PARK

The park was first opted for purchase by the state as an open space in 1853 and a competition was launched for the design. It was won by Frederick Law Olmsted and Calvert Vaux, who converted nearly 850 acres (344ha) of wasteland into a veritable wonderland. There are several lakes and ponds, and in the north of the park is a reservoir circled by New York's foremost public running track.

Although it is an urban park, with masses of statuary and such formal features as the **Bethesda Fountain** and terrace and the **Belvedere Castle**, there's lots of green space from the **Ramble** to the **Great Lawn** and **Sheep Meadow**. At the northern end is the formal **Conservatory Garden**.

At 64th Street look for the newly revamped **Central Park Zoo**, which used to be free and rundown, but now they charge for its new look. There's a small collection of animals and a popular seal pool. Cars are banned at weekends.

Very popular and with plenty to do, in Central Park you can walk, jog, cycle or even ride; there's Shakespeare at the **Delacorte Theater** in summer and tennis on the courts near the reservoir. It's open all year round, but don't go at night, or wander around deserted places.

Buildings in Central Park

It's estimated that if all the constructions planned for Central Park by well-meaning (and some more commercially inclined) folk were built, the entire space between 59th Street and 110th would have been built over almost twice by now. Fortunately, there's a strong movement to keep the park green, but buildings that have elbowed in include the **Metropolitan Museum of Art**, the **Arsenal**, the **Zoo**, the **Delacorte Theater**, the **Tavern on the Green**, various stables, boat-houses and bandstands and a police station.

See Map D–I4 | ★★★

FRICK COLLECTION

In the USA museums are often palatial buildings – as in Philadelphia, Boston and even Detroit. The ones built by the merchant barons of the 19th and early 20th centuries are stellar, and New York is no exception. This one is a star in the city's museum firmament: the kingly marble palace of Henry Clay Frick, a coal merchant whose mines made him a fortune. He was hardly cultured, but he was wisely advised to use the talents of a top New York and London dealer, Lord Duveen, ever-anxious to sell European works of art to rich American patrons.

It is actually quite a small building, in a splendid position facing Central Park, and it is quite possible to see it in a couple of hours. But it would be a pity not to linger before the marvellous sculptures and lavish interior decors. The famous well-spaced paintings ranging from **Titian** to **Whistler** include **Rembrandt's** *Polish Rider* and **Vermeer's** *Officer and the Laughing Girl*, the rare **Dürer** portrait and **Gainsborough's** *Mall in St James's Park*. The collection is indeed of the finest pictures to be seen. No wonder then that a social leader (supposedly Nancy Cunard), visiting when the Frick was new, was heard to murmur 'Oh my God, how Duveen!' It's a major draw, both for its art and the building itself, even if the latter can seem rather like a very luxurious funeral parlour!

The Frick Collection
1 East 70th Street at Fifth Avenue, NYC 10021
212 288 0700
info@frick.org
www.frick.org
10:00–18:00 Tue–Sat (to 21:00 Fri), 13:00–18:00 Sun
M1, M2, M3, M4, M30, M66, M72
M train 6

Opposite: *Central Park is a green haven in the concrete jungle.*
Below: *Holbein's portrait of Sir Thomas More is one of the Frick's gems.*

Chrysler Building
✉ 405 Lexington Avenue, at 42nd Street, NYC 10017 (access to foyer only)
🚌 M42, M101, M102, M103, M104
M trains: 4, 5, 6, 7

See Map E–C3 ★★

CHRYSLER BUILDING

A slender and impressive monument to **Art Deco**, much loved by New Yorkers, this famous skyscraper at Lexington and 42nd is the Chrysler Building. It was constructed as the New York headquarters and additionally as a praise-poem to the Chrysler motor car. This enduring monument to the motor car is appropriately adorned with all sorts of decorative elements from grilles and ornaments to hub caps, friezes of 1930s motor cars, and symbols of energy. These are particularly noticable at night when the sleek grey-blue Chrysler bursts into dazzling light. It's unique, yet a typical example of New York's wonderful sense of excess in high Art Deco. Go inside and see the lobbies and the interior fittings.

This was New York's first 'modern' skyscraper, and for a time (just one year) the 77-storey building plus spire held the proud title of the 'tallest building in the world' until trumped by the Empire State. Apparently skyscrapers sway – they have to or they would tumble. But it is still a shock when you are shown a clothes closet on a high floor here: even on a calm day the hanging coats all move on their racks.

Below: *The 1930s live on. Hidden during construction, the crowning needle was produced on completion of the Chrysler building.*

See Map D–F5 | ★★

CATHEDRAL OF ST JOHN THE DIVINE

Above: *The rose window of St John the Divine, New York's mammoth Anglican cathedral.*

Beside Morningside Park, this enormous cathedral is situated at 112th Street and Amsterdam Avenue. It dominates the neighbourhood, and this Gothic edifice shouldn't be missed. As New York's Anglican cathedral, it is reputedly bigger than Notre Dame and Chartres and, although begun in 1892 and having survived changes of style, it's still not finished. There are several attractions within, from an ancient fossil to an altar dedicated to AIDS victims.

A fascinating place to visit on weekdays is the studio where masons and sculptors work on the pieces needed to construct and decorate the building. The cathedral is being built on traditional lines and the masons can be seen at work in the **Stonecutting Yard**.

Many works of art have been given to the Anglican cathedral and can be seen on a rotating basis in its museum.

Aside from regular Anglican religious services, with notable music and choral works, St John's is also a cultural centre with a busy schedule of secular events, and there are bound to be theatre or dance performances and exhibitions when you visit. It's a lively place, and a concert here is a lovely experience. In the neighbouring **Children's Sculpture Garden** is a curious fountain and a display of works by local schoolchildren.

Cathedral of St John the Divine
⊠ 1047 Amsterdam Avenue, at 112 Street, NYC 10025
www.stjohndivine.org
07:00–17:00 daily
M4, M11, M60, M104
M trains 1, 9

See Map E–G3 ★★

Above: *Unlike its neighbours, Chinatown grows and keeps burgeoning.*

CHINATOWN

This is one of the most fascinating areas of New York. Chinatown, at the southern edge of the Lower East Side, is many things to many people and one thing is sure: you can eat very well indeed here. But this is New York, so forget the large and well ordered Chinese communities in London, Vancouver or San Francisco. This one is, by comparison, a mess.

It's fearfully crowded and grimy, but what a place – it's both smelly and sophisticated, and it is real. Some 150,000 Chinese live and work between the confines of the Bowery and Broadway, and many of their relations from all over town come 'back home' on weekends. Originally a defined area, it is bursting at the seams.

The heart of the community is **Mott Street**, a restaurant alley. Though the area is mainly Cantonese you can find excellent Shanghai, Pekingese and Szechwan style food. You can also eat from stalls and fill up on intriguing snacks. Eating can be a real bargain here, with plenty of choice and lots of special menus displayed to lure you in.

There are many dim sum restaurants. These give you a chance to sample tiny servings, often hot, often spicy, of a range of sometimes mysterious specialities. You are charged by the dish, usually piled up in little baskets. Dim sum houses serve from morning to mid-afternoon. Other places go

Chinatown Museum

If you want to know more about the Chinese, see the displays of Sino- American history, photographs of Chinese life in the USA, or take a walking tour of the area, then go to the **Museum of Chinese in the Americas** on Mulberry and Bayard. This is an interesting centre for serious study of the phenomenon of Chinatown. There is a library that can be used and a bookshop.

✉ 70 Mulberry St
☎ 212 619 4785
Fax 212 619 4720
info@moca-nyc.org
www.moca-nyc.org

See Map A–A3 | ★★

from cheap to charming, decorated with gilded dragons, fans, flowers, lanterns and figurines. Go at night when multicoloured neon signs compete with each other.

Shops selling the usual Oriental merchandise – scrolls and silk shoes and saucepans to kites and cricket cages and chopsticks – are sandwiched in the narrow streets. Upstairs rooms are often clubrooms. There's a temple with gilt buddhas on Mott Street, as well as the Chinatown Fair (an amusement arcade), which used to have a famous curiosity: dancing and game-playing live chickens. Chinatown is a place with a life of its own, and even the telephone booths are capped with painted and gilded pagodas.

Ellis Island
☎ 212 363 3206
www.ellisisland.com
09:30–17:00 daily
Go from Battery Park by ferry

ELLIS ISLAND

This is a national monument to the more than 17 million New Americans who arrived here between 1892 and 1954. A major refurbishment has provided this one-time entry point with attractions dealing with the island's adaptation and also a complete history of the new arrivals. It touchingly retells the story of the great immigration which began in the mid-19th century; note the promenade beside a wall of commemoration with the names of no fewer than 400,000 American immigrants.

Below: *These stern halls on an isolated island once confronted all immigrants. Now they house a fascinating museum on this vital aspect of US history.*

American Museum of Natural History
☒ Central Park West at 79th Street, NYC 10024
☎ 212 769 5100
www.amnh.org
daily
M1, M2, M3, M4, M30, M66, M72, M101, M102, M103
M trains: 1, 9, B, C
restaurant and snack bar

Lincoln Center for the Performing Arts
☒ Columbus Ave between 62nd and 66th
☎ 212 874 5350
M5, M7, M11, M66, M104
M trains: 1, 9

See Map D–H5 ★★

AMERICAN MUSEUM OF NATURAL HISTORY

This is the largest natural history museum in the world. There are new state-of-the art dinosaur halls, displays of animals living and extinct, ocean life, birds and all sorts of stones from gems to meteorites. Although most of the four-level structure is resolutely old-style with cavernous halls and wide tiled passages, there have been many changes. A vast modern cube to the rear contains a new Planetarium – the Rose Center is a new facility for Earth and Space IMAX films.

Forty halls show the diversity of life through the universe. Temporary shows focus on news and pictures from contrasting areas of the globe, and there is a lively show of butterflies. There is a restaurant, though it's a pity the large snack bar (with good healthy food and drink) is buried in a windowless basement, for the museum is surrounded by a lovely park with lots of places to sit, facing onto Central Park itself. Consider having a picnic in warm weather. There are lots of food shops along the nearby main avenues.

Of the older attractions the beautifully maintained dioramas of wildlife, particularly in Africa, are a perfect way to imagine animal and bird life in that fascinating continent. There are guided tours, educational programmes and lectures, and gift shops.

Below: *One of the exhibits at the American Museum of Natural History.*

See Map E–A5 ★★

LINCOLN CENTER

Above: *The plaza of the Lincoln Center; the Met has more than 3000 seats for its opera and ballet seasons.*

A grand gesture on the part of the city brought music, opera, dance and theatre together on one plaza in a central location.

The new premises of the **Metropolitan Opera** (or 'the Met') opened in 1966 and it's still one of the smartest places at which to be seen. Standing right at the focus of the Lincoln Center plaza, its high white arches give glimpses of the grand red-carpeted staircase and the Chagall murals within. The oil company Texaco sponsors opera broadcasts and these are played over the airwaves to the nation on Saturday afternoons.

The Lincoln Center is regally flanked by **The New York State Theater** – home to the world-famous **New York City Ballet** and **New York City Opera** – and **Avery Fisher Hall**. Jazz is a regular attraction now. Drama is housed at the **Vivian Beaumont Theater**. Also here is the **Dorothy and Lewis B. Cullman Center** (New York Public Library for the Performing Arts), well worth a visit by theatre fans for its huge collection of theatre, dance, opera tapes, videos, manuscripts – and books.

The Lincoln Center is a handsome sight in pale marble grouped around a glimmering fountain. Between Avery Fisher Hall and the Juilliard are some modern sculptures, including a Henry Moore.

The Juilliard School of Music

You can visit this well-known school for professional musicians, singers and actors beside **Lincoln Center** for student performances or recitals at the **Alice Tully Hall**. Some of America's best talents are nursed here. Aside from some of its alumni, it was briefly famous in the early 1970s when the great diva, **Maria Callas**, gave a short series of masterclasses here.

See Map A–B1 | ★

Above: *Interior view of an exhibition hall at the Cloisters.*

THE CLOISTERS

Fort Tryon Park is one of Frederick Law Olmsted's creations and has at its centrepiece old **Fort Tryon** which saw service in the War of Independence. But the most famous attraction is the museum, **The Cloisters**. Here, in its elegant and cool surroundings, are numerous medieval treasures from the **Metropolitan Museum of Art**. It's a wonderful collection and is easily reached by subway to 190th Street followed by a pleasant walk through the park. You can also take a direct bus from the Met itself on Fifth Avenue.

The building appears to be an authentic 13th-century edifice, but is actually comprised of bits of old French and Spanish monasteries which were sometimes lifted wholesale from their ancient sites – it was not only the Germans who pilfered whole chunks of buildings for Berlin museums. In a thoughtful way the original designers have made the various medieval showpieces look quite at home in this sylvan setting. And they are well cared for and protected – not always the case in their far-off homes. Take plenty of time for a slow exploration and maybe a picnic in the park here. You can use your Metropolitan Museum ticket if it is for the same day, otherwise there is a suggested admission. There is also a gift shop.

The Cloisters
✉ Fort Tryon Park, at 200th Street between Broadway and the Hudson, NYC 10040
☎ 212 923 3700
🕒 09:30–17:15 Tue-Sun (16:45 in winter).
💰 children free
🚌 M4
M train A

See Map E–C4 ★

NEW YORK PUBLIC LIBRARY

At one of the city's busiest intersections stands a grande dame of a building, the handsome Public Library. A popular meeting place is the flight of steps up to its impressive entry. It has a vast repository of documents, art, letters and books, and there are frequent special exhibitions. The New York Public Library is a reference, and not a lending library (there are 80 branches around the city for that) but you are welcome to visit.

Built in stone in grandiose Beaux-Arts style, the Library is as opulent within as without and has a vast entry hall. You ascend the baronial marble staircase to the vast Reading Room on the third floor. Be sure to ask about a free tour and remember to look out for the fountains and the pair of lions guarding the steps outside. Bryant Park, the Library's 'back garden', is a place to rest, read, snack: *see* panel, page 40.

New York Public Library
✉ Fifth Avenue at 42nd, NYC 10018
☎ 212 221 7676
💻 www.nypl.org
🕒 Mon–Sat, hours vary
💰 there are frequent remarkable and usually free exhibitions

Below: *New York Public Library is a revered monument located at 42nd and Fifth Avenue.*

Places of Worship

Grace Church

This lovely church was founded at a time when the area was still a smart place to live. It is hard to credit now, but there are still elegant brick houses on the cross streets around this imposing church on Broadway and 10th Street. Built mainly to serve wealthy Episcopal parishioners, the ornate steeple, recently restored, is a local land-mark. A later marble addition replaced the wooden one even though it was thought that it would be too heavy for the church. Begun in 1843 and built in Gothic Revival style, this church gained for its designer, James Renwick, the contract to build the new St Patrick's Roman Catholic cathedral (*see* page 21) . He was only 23 when he designed Grace Church yet it is considered to be his finest achievement.

⊠ *802 Broadway at 12th Street*

☎ *212 254 2000*

Temple Emanuel-El

You don't have to be Jewish to appreciate this synagogue, the biggest in the USA seating 2500. A brooding Romanesque structure, it's full of Eastern detail.

⊠ *1 East 65th Street, NYC 10021*

☎ *212 744 1400*

🚌 *M1, M2, M3, M4, M30, M66, M72*

M *6, F, N, R, W*

St Nicholas Russian Orthodox Cathedral

On the Upper East Side you will see the onion domes of this Russian Orthodox cathedral, which adds a note of exoticism to the city.

⊠ *155 97th Street at 5th Avenue*

☎ *212 289 1915*

More places of worship on pages 21 and 27.

Museums and Galleries

Museum of the American Indian

Behind the ornate

façade of the United States Custom House on Bowling Green lies this interesting museum, with one of the largest collections of material concerning Native Americans in the world. It is part of the Smithsonian Institution and is a fascinating repository of artefacts from most of the hundreds of tribes that once inhabited the huge area we now know as the United States.

✉ *Custom House, Bowling Green, NYC 10004*
☎ *212 514 3700*
🕒 *every day except Christmas*
💻 *www.americanindian.sl.edu*
💰 *admission free*
🚌 *M1, M6, M9*
M *1, 4, 5, 9, R, W*

Lower East Side Tenement Museum

First built in 1856 on Orchard Street as the immigrant wave grew, this apartment building was one of many first homes for New Americans and is now listed as a National Historic Landmark. Within, you will find apartments of the era, some left exactly as they were when landlords turned the key on departing residents a century ago. The museum is accessible by guided tours only.

✉ *90 Orchard Street, NYC 10002*
☎ *212 431 0233*
💻 *www.tenement.org*
🕒 *13:00–16:00 Tue–Fri, 11:00–16:30 Sat–Sun.*
💰 *under 5s free*
🚌 *M9, M14A, M15*
M *J, M, Z*

Pierpont Morgan Library

Closed for several years until 2006 for renovations, this one-time palatial family

New York's First St Patrick's

St Patrick's Cathedral (*see* page 21), an exercise in Gothic Revival completed in 1888, stands in splendour on Fifth Avenue and provides an oasis for visitors from the hurry of the avenue outside. But it isn't the first St Patrick's in the city – to find that one you need to go to Little Italy on the Lower East Side and search out St Patrick's at 264 Mulberry Street. Here, damaged by fire in 1866, a bit forlorn and needing a facelift, is the Gothic Revival original of 1815, seat of the first Catholic Archbishop of New York.

Opposite: *Temple Emanuel-El has a notable Romanesque façade.*
Below: *The Museum of the American Indian shows a vast range of Native American artefacts.*

Storage
A problem shared by all New Yorkers is where to put things. The museums have the same difficulty – multiplied several times. Not all works in big collections merit display; some are only available in private study areas. Reflect, as you wander around the vast collection at the Met, that nine-tenths of the museum's holdings are reputedly housed in a storage tunnel under Fifth Avenue!

home, now a famous marble temple to the arts, has many fresh aspects. It has new spaces to show its treasures which include rare books and manuscripts, music scores, jewels. There's a new entry on Park Avenue.

✉ *29 East 36th Street*
☎ *212 685 0610*
💻 *www.morganlibrary.org*
🕒 *Usually open Tue–Sun, it is closed for renovation until 2006.*

New York Historical Society

This was New York's original museum, and many things deposited here originally found their way to the new Metropolitan when it opened. By Central Park, it's a city house, with much material on the history of the city, as well as decorative arts, and rare pictures including a range of original Audubon birds.

✉ *170 Central Park West, NYC 10024*
☎ *212 873 3400*
💻 *www.nyhistory.org*
🕒 *closed Mon*
💰 *Admission is charged, but children are free*
🚌 *M10 M72*
M *B and C trains*

Below: *Frank Lloyd Wright liked to shock and his Guggenheim Museum is controversial in its design.*

American Folk Art Museum

Down the street from the MoMA building, and often overlooked as a result, is the newly housed American Folk Art Museum. Founded in 1956 by the American Craft Council, the building was specially designed for the purpose, and its permanent collection today contains

thousands of craft artefacts – ranging from teapots to chairs to baskets to rugs – displayed on four storeys. The library next door has a fine collection of children's books.

✉ *45 West 53rd Street*
☎ *212 265 1040*
💻 *www.folkart museum.org*
🕒 *11:30–19:30 Tue–Sun.*

Solomon R Guggenheim Museum

The Guggenheim is a controversial building (some people dislike it) which was designed by Frank Lloyd Wright and is his only building in New York City. It is shaped like a flower pot and consists of descending ramps loaded with abstract and impressionist paintings by artists such as Picasso, Braque, Van Gogh and Chagall.

✉ *1071 5th Avenue at 89th Street, NY 10128*
☎ *212 423 3500*
🕒 *10:00–17:45 Sat–Wed, 10:00–20:00 Fri*
💰 *voluntary donation for last two hours on Fridays*

Whitney Museum of American Art

This museum is uncompromisingly modern and filled with American art, the gift of Mrs Gertrude Vanderbilt Whitney. Look for work by Calder, Warhol, Pollock, De Kooning, O'Keeffe and many other 20th- and 21st-century artists. It hosts lots of special art, film and video shows.

✉ *75th and Madison, and there's a midtown Whitney at Altria, Park Ave and 42nd Street*
☎ *917 663 2453*
🕒 *11:00–18:00 Wed, Thu and Sat; 13:00–18:00 Sun, 13:00–21:00 Fri*
💰 *voluntary donation for last three hours on Fridays.*

The Children's Museum of Manhattan

This museum is a fascinating experience for children, where they learn through play. There is a multimedia show and hi-tech equipment.

✉ *Tisch Building, 212 West 83rd Street, NY 10024*
☎ *212 721 1223*
💻 *www.cmom.org*
🕒 *closed Mon*
🚌 *M5, M7, M11, M79, M86, M104*
M *1, 9*

El Museo del Barrio 'Caribbean'

This museum, dedicated to the arts of Latin America and Puerto Rico, has a permanent collection of interesting pre-Columbian artefacts. With its roots in what used to be called Spanish Harlem, this lively place also offers changing exhibitions and children's events.

✉ *Fifth Avenue and 104th, NY 10029*
☎ *212 831 7272*
💻 *www.elmuseo.org*
🕒 *11:00– 17:00 Wed–Sun*
💰 *under 12s free*
🚌 *M1, M2, M3,*

Tallest in New York
Over the decades several buildings have claimed to be the tallest in the world, only to lose the title to another even taller construction. The first of these was the Flatiron, then came the Chrysler in 1930, which was competing with the Bank of Manhattan and pipped it to the post by adding a surprise spire at the last minute. A year later it was spiked by the Empire State which held the coveted title for over 40 years. It is again the tallest since the destruction of the World Trade Towers. Discussions still go on to decide what will eventually rise here.

Architectural Remnants
The loss of Penn Station, a grand building, was much mourned (trains are now under Madison Square Garden). Next to the lost original stands the old classical post office, which may become the new train station. A century ago 6th Avenue up from 14th Street was the shopping street and you can still see remnants of the Classical Revival façades typical of the period, pillared and decorated with flowers and foliage.

M4, M106
M *2, 3, 6*

More museums on pages 19, 23, 25, 29, 30 and 32.

Historical Sites

Ground Zero

The towers of the World Trade Center once dominated Manhattan's skyline – the PATH line dramatically circles the site. Walk along by the gravestones of the defiant St Paul's Chapel to see developments, look through windows overlooking the site. Or best of all, at the World Financial Center view it from the dazzling high glass atrium of the Winter Garden. Here are shops and cafés often offering concerts – an exotic, palm-shaded place for a stroll or a drink and a place to appreciate the busy harbour too.

✉ *Check National Parks Service*
☎ *718 354 4606*
💻 *www.nps.gov/nycparks*

Castle Clinton National Monument

Like its twin, Castle William, on Governor's Island at the East Battery, Castle Clinton was built in 1808 to protect the city. When peace and independence made the fortress redundant, it was roofed over and became a music hall. Among the stars of the day who performed here, the 'Swedish nightingale', Jenny Lind, sang here in 1850 – it was her American debut. In 1896 Castle Clinton became the New York Aquarium (now in Brooklyn) but today is a National Historic Monument with exhibits on the history of New York.

✉ *Battery Park, NYC 2004*
☎ *212 344 7220*
🕒 *08:30–17:00 daily.*

Old Merchant's House

This unusual Federal-style residence was fortunately saved

from destruction. It's a solitary example of what many of the city's streets once looked like, and of how affluent families lived during the 19th century. The house is over 160 years old and has been carefully renovated as a typical family home of the period.

✉ *29 East 4th Street, NYC 10003*
☎ *212 777 1080*
💻 *www.merchants house.com*
🕒 *13:00–17:00 Thu–Mon, closed Tue–Wed*
💰 *admission charge*
🚌 *M1, M8, M103*
M *6, B, D, F, N, R, V, W*

The Flatiron Building

Although 22 floors doesn't seem much to us today, this building was a monster in 1902 when it loomed over Fifth Avenue. It was then the biggest skyscraper in New York! Built to conform to a triangular plot at the angle of Broadway and Fifth, this grand old New York survivor is a prestigious office tower, and is now protected from the wreckers as it has been designated a City Landmark.

✉ *175 5th Avenue at 23rd St, NYC 10010*
☎ *212 477 0947*

Theodore Roosevelt's Birthplace

The President's birthplace is hardly imposing, being one of a row of brownstone buildings from 1840. No. 28 has five rooms reflecting the style of the President's childhood. His family moved when he was 15 years old.

✉ *Just off Broadway on East 20th Street,*
☎ *212 260 1616*
🕒 *09:00–17:00 Tue–Sat*

Green Spaces

Gramercy Park

Although the actual place that this name applies to is a small East Side garden square at the foot of Lexington Avenue between 20th and

The Vanished City

Much of Lower Manhattan has vanished, including major skyscrapers such as the Singer Building, a domed tower in the Beaux-Arts style, the Tribune Building, and many small and often elegant warehouses and loft buildings. It's worth getting a picture book showing Lower Manhattan as it was 30 years ago. Since then whole streets have vanished, so take a camera and record your visit. Next time the view won't be the same!

Below: *The Flatiron Building, an early and impressively sited skyscraper.*

Bryant Park
One of New York's success stories, this space behind the library along 42nd Street has been reclaimed from the sad place it was and is a charming garden once again. The terrace café along its rear wall is a delight, and it is again pleasant to stroll among the flowerbeds. Bryant Park housed a Crystal Palace built for the world's fair in 1853. There's a discount ticket booth at the Sixth Avenue exit, an old merry-go-round or carousel to one side. A busy Christmas market with lots of stalls takes place here every year.

21st Streets, Gramercy Park's name resounds far beyond the 60 dwellings located on the square. It is a very smart address to have. The buildings edging the square were designed by some of the best-known architects. People living around the actual garden have keys to it. A century and a half after it was created, Gramercy Park is now the only private garden of its kind in the city.

Battery Park

At the foot of Manhattan Island is Battery Park, a green space of 35 acres based on infill with a mile long esplanade. Now 92 acres, since the reclaiming and greening of the ruined West Side highway sites, Battery Park has been the southern focus of a splendid extensive ribbon development, which still continues. With wide views of the Hudson and the harbour, there are gardens, play spaces, public art and regular free events. The park takes its name from the line-up of cannons once surmounting the nearby circular stone fort. Boats leave for the Statue of Liberty, Ellis Island and Staten Island from the park's docks.

✉ *2 South End Ave, NYC 10280*
☎ *212 267 9700*
💻 *www.bpcparks.org*

More green spaces on pages 22 and 24.

Right: *Hope Garden in Battery Park.*

Left: *Aspiring baseball stars playing America's popular summer sport.*

ACTIVITIES

Sport and Recreation

New York is a major centre for all sports, though the popular ones such as **baseball** (April–October) and **American Football** (August–December) are outstanding. The Mets (the local baseball team) meet at Shea Stadium (Roosevelt Avenue in Flushing), the New York Yankees at Yankee Stadium in the Bronx. Football is played at the Giants' Stadium in Rutherford, New Jersey and the teams are the Giants and the Jets. Note that tickets for these events are very hard to come by.

Basketball, also very popular, (November to April) has one main team, the Knickerbockers, or 'Knicks', who play at Madison Square Garden. **Ice Hockey** teams (October to April) are the New York Rangers and the New Jersey Devils, the former at Madison Square Garden.

Other sports are available to the visitor in bewildering array. You can go bowling or boating, running or rollerblading, swimming or skating. You can play golf, squash or tennis, and there are fitness classes on

Shea Stadium
✉ 123–01 Rooosevelt Avenue (126th Street in Queens), Flushing, 11368
☎ 718 507 8499
🖳 www.mets.com

Yankee Stadium
✉ 161 Street at River Avenue, Bronx, 10451
☎ 718 293 6000
🖳 www.yankees.com

Giants' Stadium
✉ East Rutherford NJ Stadium, NJ 07073
☎ 201 935 8222
🖳 www.njsea.com
🖳 www.giants.com
🖳 www.newyorkjets.com

Madison Square Garden
✉ 4 Penn Plaza (31st–33rd streets on 7th Avenue, NYC 10001
☎ info: 212 465 6741, tickets: 212 307 7171
🖳 www.thegarden.com

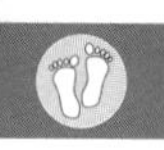

Right: *Taking a slow mooch by horse-drawn carriage through Central Park is a popular thing to do.*

offer all over town. There's horse riding in Central Park and in Brooklyn, as well as several race tracks (*see* panel, page 74). Riding and exercise trails in Brooklyn and the suburbs can be found in the city's parks and beaches.

You can do almost anything in the city's **parks** – New York claims to have more green space than any other American city. In the big ones such as Manhattan's Central Park and others in Brooklyn and the Bronx are well-maintained areas for exercise. The ribbon of land on the Manhattan side of the Hudson River down from the 50s has many sports facilities from biking and acrobatics to golf practise drives and tennis courts. And the green development continues: in the extended Battery Park for example are fresh facilities to enhance new hotels and housing developments – a mile long esplanade as well as sport and play spaces, public art, regular free events. Your efforts can be soothing too – taking the cool evening air on a carriage ride through Central Park is a classic, or simply sit in the sun and practise your yoga!

Fitness

There are lots of young New Yorkers! Despite the many problems of living in a city like this, from exorbitant rents to the high cost of living, they still keep coming. One thing New Yorkers of all ages seem to love is keeping fit. To serve their needs dozens of health clubs have sprung up in all the boroughs, offering gym fit ideas and slimming courses, as well as steam and massage treatments. To have your own personal trainer is a big thing. Hardly a hotel opens nowadays without its own pool or health centre, so even if you're just passing through, you won't lose out.

Alternative New York

Sex in the City

It may not be advertised as such in brochures and tourist information, but as a city, New York also sells sex. It is available here even though the city authorities continually attempt to 'clean it up'. There's even a museum of sex at Fifth Avenue and East 27th Street – opened in 2003, it's quite a lure. Prostitutes used to swarm in the theatre district – now cleaned up – and they have moved to Lower Manhattan and the lorry parks in Brooklyn. The crack sellers still crouch in alleys off Eighth Avenue.

Exotically dressed, some of the 'girls' are transvestites. Boys are also available along some avenues and in a number of East and West Side bars; at the Gaiety Club on West 46th Street, naked studs strip and show. For voyeurs there are sex-cinemas (along midtown Eighth Avenue) with hard-core films. There are live sex shows too, even on Broadway. In New York anything goes, and liberal laws means that if someone wants it, you can find it here. But take care if you walk or drive through some neighbourhoods as theft and sometimes violence are not uncommon. And it should go without saying that if you do participate, take condoms: safe sex is 'de rigueur'.

Do you want to try something completely different? Spawned by the TV show, there's even a *Sex and the City* tour on offer.

Hayden Planetarium
Adjoining the **Natural History Museum** is the exciting new Frederick Phineas and Sandra Priest Rose Center for Earth and Space, containing what is still generally called the **Hayden Planetarium**, where you can see magical views of the heavens. Both museums are ideal for family visits. The new **AOL Time Warner Center** has 'cultural space' as well as shops and restaurants.

Below: *A renewed police presence in New York helps to make the visitors feel more confident.*

Walking Tours

Museums of Lower Manhattan
www.NYstartshere.org

Municipal Art Society
212 935 3960
www.mas.org

#1 New York City Tours
702 233 1627
www.1newyorkcitytours.com

NYC Tours
Free nature walks.
0800 201 7275

Walking Tours

New York is very much a walking city. That is if you are thinking Manhattan, for the other four boroughs are less tightly packed and urban. Brooklyn has much to offer, central Queens and the Bronx can be like villages, and Staten Island is as close to the country as New York City gets.

Guided Walking and Museum Tours

Do you enjoy getting out and discovering a new place on foot? If you want to be included in a like-minded group then a walking tour of the city is an ideal way to discover its pleasures. There are several general ones, but you may also choose specific subjects, such as museums, theatreland, historical, literary. There's even one for nature walks, and some are offered in Italian, Spanish and Portuguese.

Museum walks are popular, and concentrated ones can include such stars as the **Metropolitan** (*see* page 23), the **Frick** (*see* page 25), the **Guggenheim** (*see* page 37), the German-Austrian **Neue Galerie** and the **Goethe Institute**, as well as the Spanish **Museo del Barrio** (*see* page 37), all ranged along 5th Avenue. Another well contrasted set is in lower Manhattan and can include up to 15 institutions. These range from the Smithsonian's **Museum of the American Indian** (*see* page 35) to the **South Street Seaport Museum** (*see* page 20), the **Museum of Immigration**

Below: *South Street Seaport Museum is a really lively evocation of 19th-century life in New York.*

on Ellis Island (including the **Statue of Liberty** – *see* page 15) and even the **New York City Police Museum**. You can also take tours to the museums of the Bronx, Brooklyn and Queens – there's even a Coney Island Museum!

Other themes, such as the **theatre** and **Central Park** (*see* page 24) and its history, are also mainly local. **Broadway** and its cluster of show places around the West 40s is very popular and the distances are short and easy. There are special organizations to help with all of these (*see* panel, page 44). Or you can request a personally conducted one with your own list of 'must sees'. Most tours are wheelchair friendly too.

Neighbourhood tours are always interesting and you could walk the streets of **Greenwich Village** (*see* page 22) or **Brooklyn Heights**. The new developments along the **Hudson** and its rescued piers makes for extended self-guided walks which you can join at any point.

For these tours all you need are good shoes, an umbrella, protective clothing, and an adventurous spirit of course.

Above: *Central Park's space is sacrosanct. It could so easily have been built over, and lost.*

Museums
Most of the city's museums gained their treasures from private collections. The rich New Yorkers are often commemorated with the names of individual galleries or extensions to the buildings. However, aside from grand galleries, many small museums can easily go unremarked in the city. If you have a specialist interest, in anything ranging from dolls to railway memorabilia, chances are there is a collection for you.

Above: *A new Fifth Avenue face is the Trump Tower.*

Architectural Styles
The style of the Greek Revival, last seen in the early 19th century, returned in the early 20th century. Alas, Pennsylvania Station, a grandiose Greek temple, has gone, replaced by **Madison Square Garden**, but you can still feel those expansive times in the marble halls of **Grand Central Terminal** on East 42nd Street. Later came many upshooting buildings (both the **Empire State** and the **Chrysler** buildings, elegant epitomes of the **Art Deco** style, date from this time). New building and the desire to impress resulted in architectural booms with New York being a mirror of many architectural styles.

Manhattan Architecture

If you're interested in architecture, Manhattan is a walker's joy. True, it means a lot of walking on hard surfaces, and watching out too while you gaze up – for Manhattan invites 'rubber-necking'. (To save your feet there are open-top tour buses that allow easier viewing.) As you pass the taller buildings you can't help craning – sometimes it seems that the developers, particularly of older buildings, only allowed their imagination to run riot on the upper floors. In Lower Manhattan sculpted or applied decoration often covers constructions, from Beaux Arts to Art Deco, and the façades of smaller buildings too. There were also flirtations with classical styles: examples are the vanished block-long **Penn Station** (don't miss the photographs in the concourse under Madison Square Gardens) or the classical columns of the **Post Office** opposite.

The architecture of the city is one of the pleasures of being here. And it's not all a tall tale. True, there is very little left of 18th-century Manhattan, but some samples

from the elegant 19th-century building boom still exist (*see* **The Merchant's House**, page 39.) **Brownstones** in whole terraces of this typical stone exist along midtown and uptown streets. Harlem has some particularly fine examples. The cast-iron façades of Lower Manhattan factories and storehouses are famous.

However, it was in the late 19th and 20th centuries that New York came into flower. From baronial buildings such as **City Hall** to weird wonders like the **Trump Tower**, from early medium high risers such as those by East 23rd Street to modern shafts like the **UN Building**, from the cute to the commanding, it's all here. In New York new things are admired, and here the modern can be marvellous too.

Cruises
You can make the best of fine weather by taking cruises to circumnavigate Manhattan Island, or simply enjoy an evening of dancing and drinking. Some options are:

Staten Island Ferry
☎ 718 727 2508

Zephyr
One-hour tours of lower Manhattan harbour from South Street Seaport.
☎ 212 269 5755.

New York Water Taxi
☎ 212 742 1969

See also panel, page 17.

Organized Tours

From coach tours to walks, from helicopter flights to cruises around the harbour, there are lots of possibilities. It's a good idea to check with tourist offices for local trips and ideas. Try **Circle Lines** and **New York Water-**

Below: *The open-topped tour bus service is useful for your first visit to Manhattan.*

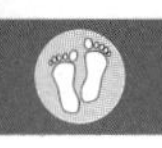

Loeb Boathouse
☎ 212 517 3623

Gray Line of New York
✉ 777 8th Ave, 10036
☎ 212 445 0848

Shortline Bus Tours
✉ 166 West 46th Street
☎ 212 354 5122.

Harlem Spirituals Inc
✉ 690 8th Avenue, near Times Square, or 1457, 1697 Broadway
☎ 212 391 0900

Harlem Heritage Tours
✉ 230 West 116th Street, NYC 10026
☎ 212 280 7888

New York Limo Tours
☎ 702 233 1627

Liberty Helicopter
✉ West 30th Street and 12th Avenue,
☎ 212 967 6464

Ponycabs
✉ 517 Broome Street,
☎ 212 766 9222

Hayden Planetarium
✉ Rose Center, Central Park West at 79th Street, NYC 10024
🕒 12:30–16:45 daily

Brooklyn Museum
✉ 200 Eastern Parkway, Brooklyn 11238
☎ 718 638 5000
💻 www.brooklyn museum.org

way for exploratory trips. Other craft cruise the harbour from the South Street Seaport base, or you can even charter your own. The classic harbour cruise is still the one on the Staten Island Ferry to the island and back, but there are also frequent day services out to Liberty and Ellis Islands and the sometimes open Governor's Island. Beyond New York try **Greyhound coach lines** or you can rent private cars to be driven out to Connecticut, New Jersey, Long Island and other parts of New York State.

You can rent bicycles in Central Park at the **Loeb Boathouse**. Other rental places are listed in the commercial section of the NY phone books. Or try the popular bike-powered rickshaws.

A standard day-long hop-on, hop-off tour or a quick two-hour introduction is available from **Gray Line of New York**. All day or a few hours, a variety of tours is on offer from **Shortline Bus Tours**.

Several companies offer Harlem tours which include visits to Gospel churches and a typical soul food meal. To hear some of the renowned Harlem gospel singing, try **Harlem Spirituals** or **Harlem Renaissance Tours**. The latter also visit famous places, as do **Penny Sightseeing Company**, offering walking tours with gospel singing. For an old-style jazz night in Harlem clubs, go in a stretch limo with **New York Limo Tours**. The cars wait for you until well into the wee hours before heading back downtown (reservations are necessary for limo tours).

For helicopter tours, **Liberty Helicopter** offer visitors a bird's-eye view of the city. For a romantic carriage trot around Manhattan or the park, contact **Ponycabs**.

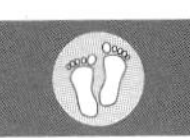

Fun for Children

Visit the new-look **American Museum of Natural History** (*see* page 30), with a parade of dinosaurs and lively programmes for children, or the **Hayden Planetarium** next door (*see* panel, page 43). Other options include the **Bronx Zoo**, with thousands of animals, reptiles and birds shown in large natural looking spaces. All six continents are represented. There's a World of Darkness show for nocturnal animals and a children's zoo.

Children will enjoy the **Brooklyn Museum** and the **Children's Museum of Manhattan** (*see* page 37). A harbour visit aboard the *Beast*, South Street Seaport's Lightship, and the four-masted *Peking* are also fun. The Zoo and the Alice in Wonderland statue in **Central Park** (*see* page 24) or the Children's Garden and fountain at **St John the Divine** (*see* page 27) are good if it's a fine day.

Intrepid Sea Air Space Museum is for lovers of classic machines, from Concorde to the great aircraft carrier *Intrepid*. With much to experience here, it is a particularly good idea for kids. It's right on the Hudson with lots of things to do. Afterwards take a walk along the new riverside belt of parkland stretching to Battery Park.

Above: *A water taxi is a great way to get the best view of Manhattan's skyline.*

Bronx Zoo
☒ Bronx River Parkway, Bronx 10460
☎ 718 367 1010
🖳 www.bronxzoo.com
🕒 08:00–18:00 Tue–Fri, 10:00–18:00 Sat–Sun; some exhibits are closed in winter.

Bronx Museum of the Arts
☒ 1040 Grand Concourse, Bronx 10456
🖳 www.bxma.org

Intrepid Sea Air Space Museum
☒ 12th Avenue at West 46th Street
☎ 212 245 0072
🖳 www.intrepidmuseum.org
🕒 daily except Mondays in winter
🚌 M42 Times Square, M50 49th Street Broadway
M Times Square or Broadway-West 49th

Right: *Saks Fifth Avenue is but one of New York's impressive department stores.*

Shopping

Where to Shop

In New York you will find **department stores**, **speciality stores** of every kind, **markets** and even **galleries**. Whatever you require, however much you have to spend, shoppers can find heaven here, and the city is also a great **fashion** centre. In many countries the dollar exchange rate is good and the amounts of cash you can bring in are considerable. In addition, almost every place in New York takes plastic, but check which credit cards are accepted before you buy. There are great **bargains** to be found here, particularly in clothes, household goods, gadgets, electrical and computer products, linens, books and CDs. You can find top labels on sale, (January sales are popular, especially along West 34th Street) or go slumming and sift through stuff on Orchard Street's stalls. Even thrift shops in the smart areas can produce good buys and offer fascinating browsing. Try Greenmarket in Union Square for fruit, bread and vegetables. Invaluable for self-caterers.

Museum Shopping

Most museums have shops selling cards, posters and bibelots. Increasingly they also have notably fine reproductions of museum treasures. The shop at the **Metropolitan Museum of Art** is very lively, particularly at festival times when along with the museum foyers and staircases it is beautifully decorated. Don't miss it at Christmas time, when there is always an enormous 'themed' Christmas tree. There are sub-branches of the museum shop at the Rockefeller Center and the South Street Seaport. For the first time since the 1970's, the museum is open on Holiday Mondays from 09:30–17:30.

Bookshops are open late and often provide a social hub for like-minded folk, not only for browsers but in their self-contained coffee shops and sitting areas. **Ursus Books,** ✉ 132 West 21st Street, ☎ 212 627 5370 (or ✉ at the Carlyle Hotel), are recommended for art books and bargains.

Main areas for general shopping are **Fifth Avenue** from 34th up to 59th, **West 34th Street** and the vast shopping malls out of the centre. These often have branches of top Fifth Avenue shops such as **Saks, Bergdorf Goodman** and **Lord and Taylor** as part of the complex. **FAO Schwarz** is a wonderland of toys for kids at 58th Street (*see* panel, page 53).

Individual stores in Manhattan, not in mainstream areas, include **Bloomingdale's**, the new **Abraham and Strauss** on A & S Plaza, Sixth Avenue and 33rd, and malls such as **Century Plaza**. On newly smart Sixth Avenue below 23rd Street you can shop at Filene's, and next door at 18th Street Old Navy stocks trendy sports and casual wear.

Discount stores line Lower Broadway, and even the Financial District has lures. Here you can find **Century 21 Discounts** (✉ 22 Cortlandt St) and many bargains at **J and R Music and Computer World** (✉ 31 Park Row). For discount fashion and more bargains try **Daffy's** (✉ 135 East 57th Street, and five other branches).

Bookshops in the City

New York has always been a book city with varied book shops, from grand stores such as the famous **Gotham Book Mart** near the Rockefeller Center to the multimillion-volume **Strand** store in the East Village. The big firms have recently become even bigger. There are several along Broadway and these are veritable social centres, offering snack bars and sitting areas. They also stay open late at night and have become places to meet friends old and new.

Below: *In SoHo many old-fashioned businesses still exist, such as this corner bookshop.*

Antiques
You might not think New York would be a place to find antiques, but this city thrives on auction sales, and serves up many surprises. There are antique marts with lots of stands here, fine for bargain hunting and browsing on a cold or damp day. Try the **Place des Antiquaires** at ⊠ 125 East 57th, or not far off ⊠ on Second Avenue, the **Manhattan Antique Center**.

New York just wouldn't be New York without **Macy's**. In this gigantic block-long, nine floor-and-basement department store you do have everything. It claims to be the largest department store in the world and even publishes its own directory. It used to have famous price wars with the departed Gimbel's, but now, the 140-year-old Macy's rules. If you aren't 'just looking' and can't find what you're after then consult the Visitor's Center which is situated on the mezzanine floor for information. You can also book for restaurants and shows here. Macy's even provides a professional shoppers' service as well as an interpretation service.

Don't overlook the **museum shops** (*see* panel, page 50). There are big ones at the Metropolitan and Museum of Modern Art, or whole shopping sections in attractions such as the South Street Seaport.

If you want to shop but don't have the time, department stores like Macy's will do it for you with your own personal shopper who will discuss your needs and then select the items or guide you to specific departments.

If you don't care for the bigger stores, Madison Avenue from 42nd Street up has a galaxy of small stylish shops. You can also try East 57th Street – a parade of expensive galleries and boutiques.

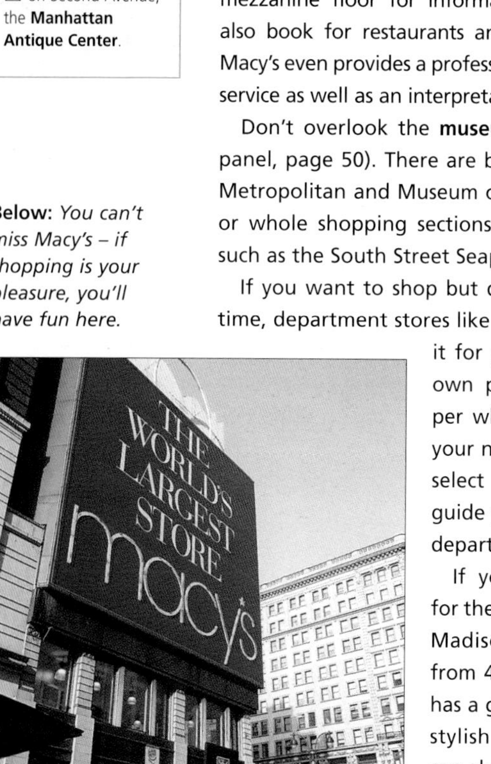

Below: *You can't miss Macy's – if shopping is your pleasure, you'll have fun here.*

Above: *Street markets selling all kinds of goods can be found everywhere.*

Food shops are plentiful on main avenues like Second, Third and Upper Broadway, but check that foodstuffs can be imported before you leave for home. Also be sure that with electrical and software goods you can use them outside the USA. (Bridge Kitchenware at ⊠ 214 East 52nd Street is helpful here.) You may need converters or adaptors. Be aware that a sizable sales tax is added to purchases.

Washington Square (*see* page 22) is enhanced by various bookshops, some of them warrens, such as The Strand which is a vast, multimillion-volumed place at 12th Street and Broadway. There are many other shops, particularly along Fourth Avenue.

The Village is the place to find items such as unusual books, clothes and foodstuffs, and there are often stalls set up on quiet sidestreets to sell fascinating things such as carvings, candles and even cult objects. If you like shopping, there are lots of opportunities to find unique items here.

If you don't mind crowds, you'll enjoy Orchard Street between Delancy Street and East Houston Street. It is the ultimate place for discount shopping for clothes, fabrics, household goods and hardware. It's busy on Sundays, as it was originally a market set up by Jewish merchants. Some shops are still shuttered on Saturdays, but new arrivals, including young designers, are reviving it.

Toy Shops

Don't even think of visiting a toy-palace like **FAO Schwarz** at ⊠ 767 Fifth Avenue at Christmas time unless you like to inflict punishment on yourself. Not only is the place crammed, but there are queues or 'line-ups' out in the cold on 58th Street waiting to get in. Once inside the place it is like a gigantic game, with salespeople dressed in costume and uniform demonstrating all the latest toys and fads. Take kids if you can, but keep a hold on the credit cards if you don't want a big bill. This one's an expensive bazaar.

Above: *The Waldorf-Astoria is a stylish, classically Art Deco grand hotel.*

WHERE TO STAY

Many possibilities exist in a range of prices, from **hostels** and **bed-and-breakfasts** to **motels** and top luxury **hotels**. It's unlikely that visitors will want to stay anywhere other than in the centre, so the following are almost all Manhattan-based suggestions, and since there are so many, this is only a short representative list of possibilities. More detailed lists can be found at **CitySearch**, or consult the **New York Travel Advisory Bureau** for occasional deals. For booking services try **Express Reservations**, or **Accommodations Express**, a seven-day-a-week free service offering room discounts. On weekends many hotels will compete to offer lower rates when business people have gone home. Check newspapers or the **NY Convention and Visitors' Bureau** for bargain weekend packages, or ask hotels when booking direct. Packages can also include tours, free meals, plus all those little extra luxuries to invite you in to fill rooms at quiet times. Bear in mind that the price quoted will not usually include the steep local NYC taxes. These may well add 13–25% plus $2 to your bill. Note that Manhattan telephone numbers are all prefixed 212, if calling long distance, but beyond the island they differ.

Another option is **Homestay New York**, a well-respected accommodation service for those who want the experience of living with real New Yorkers. Hosts are carefully screened and matched with guests.

CitySearch
www.newyork.citysearch.com

New York Travel Advisory Bureau
www.NYTAB.com

Express Reservations
www.hotelsinmanhattan.com
303 218 7608

Accommodations Express
800 444 7666

The NY Convention and Visitors' Bureau
810 Seventh Avenue, NY 10019

Homestay New York
www.homestayny.com

Midtown

• *LUXURY*

The Essex House (Map E–A4)
Located on the park with another entrance on 58th Street, this hotel has impeccable style, excellent service, and two notable restaurants. Although it is an older hotel, it has a health spa and a business centre.
✉ *160 Central Park South,* ☎ *212 247 0300,* 📠 *315 1839,* 🖱 *essexhouse.reservations@westin.com* 💻 *www.westin.com*

The Four Seasons (Map E–A3)
A huge building, palatial foyers, a good restaurant and large rooms are just some of the features of this smart address on the East Side.
✉ *57 East 57th Street,* ☎ *212 758 5700,* 📠 *758 5711,* 💻 *www.fourseasons.com/newyorkfs*

The Plaza (Map E–A4)
This is perhaps New York's most famous hotel. Facing Central Park, The Plaza is an expensive grande dame with famed bars like the Oak Room, but the rooms are not large. Although famous, it has been in the news as a ripe possibility for conversion into condominiums. It seems half of it may go that way, the rooms upgraded and famous public rooms and bars retained. Check first.
✉ *Fifth Ave, at 59th Street,* ☎ *212 759 3000,* 📠 *759 3167.*

UN Plaza (Map E–B2)
You can do something unusual here – play tennis and swim indoors, high up in the air and with views of the UN Building too!
✉ *44th at First Avenue,* ☎ *212 758 1234,* 📠 *702 5051.*

The Sheraton New York Tower (Map E–B4)
This hotel is modern, huge, and handy for Broadway theatres. Try Happy Hour drinks at the Tower Lounge.
✉ *811 Seventh Avenue,* ☎ *212 581 1000,* 📠 *262 4410,* 💻 *www.sheraton.com*

Waldorf-Astoria (Map E–B3)
On posh Park Avenue, this hotel's old-style grandeur attracts the rich and famous. Elaborately gilded Art Deco is everywhere.
✉ *301 Park Ave,* ☎ *212 355 3000,* 📠 *212 872 7272,* 💻 *www.waldorf.com*

Ritz Carlton New York Central Park (Map E–A4)
A new base for the Ritz Carlton chain, overlooking the park.
✉ *50 Central Park South,* ☎ *212 308 9100,* 📠 *212 207 8831,* 💻 *www.ritzcarlton.com/hotels/new_york_central park*

• *MID-RANGE*

The Algonquin Hotel (Map E–C4)
The Algonquin is famous and popular with writers and publishers as a shrine – the Round Table met

here (*see* panel, page 57). Alluring atmosphere, its dark-panelled lounge is good for a drink or tea.

✉ *59 West 44th,* ☎ *212 840 6800,* 📠 *212 944 1419,* 💻 *www.algonquinhotel.com*

Paramount

(Map E–B4)
Stylishly remodelled, yet retaining a 1920s atmosphere, but with rather small rooms. Near the Broadway theatres. Popular with younger business people and arts types.

✉ *235 West 46th Street,* ☎ *212 764 5500,* 📠 *212 354 5237,* 💻 *www.paramountnewyork.solmelia.com*

Wellington Hotel

(Map E–B4)
Good value, near to Broadway showplaces. A 1930s survivor, it also has a coffee shop and cocktail bar.

✉ *871 Seventh Ave,* ☎ *212 247 3900,* 📠 *581 1719,* 💻 *www.wellingtonhotel.com*

Warwick Hotel

(Map E–B4)
Located on the corner of Sixth Avenue, this welcoming, long-established hotel is ideally situated for theatre visits, Fifth Avenue shops and museums. Spacious rooms and bathrooms. Popular bar and good restaurant on ground floor. Recommended.

✉ *65 West 54th Street,* ☎ *212 247 2700,* 📠 *957 8915,* 💻 *www.warwickhotel.com*

Sherry Netherland

(Map E–A3)
Try this old-style hotel for real comfort and large rooms. Complimentary continental breakfast, newspapers, fitness centre. Located opposite Central Park.

✉ *781 5th Ave at 59th,* ☎ *212 355 2800,* 📠 *319 4306,* 💻 *www.sherrynetherland.com*

• *BUDGET*

Pickwick Arms

(Map E–B3)
Bigger than it looks, this is a reasonably priced place if you want economy in midtown. It has been newly redecorated. There's also a roof garden, and a bar is available.

✉ *230 East 51st,* ☎ *212 355 0300,* 📠 *755 5029.*

Stanford Hotel

(Map E–D4)
A small hotel that offers low prices for those on a budget and is neat and central. It is well-placed for the shops at Herald Square as well as for visiting the Javits Convention Center.

✉ *43 West 32nd,* ☎ *212 563 1500,* 📠 *629 0043.*

Aladdin Hotel

(Map E–B4)
Recently renovated and centrally located, this is a bargain option for those who don't mind shared bathrooms and dormitory-style sleeping accomodation.

✉ *317 West 45th Street,* ☎ *212 977 5700,* 📠 *246 6036.*

Wolcott Hotel

(Map E–D4)

A survival of grandiose days, this small hotel is renowned for its sculpted marble lobby – a period confection, all whipped cream and walnuts. Central location, good for shops. Well appointed rooms, free pastries and coffee at a daily lobby breakfast.

⊠ *4 West 31st St at 5th Avenue, NYC 10001,* ☎ *212 268 2900,* 📠 *212 563 0006,* 💻 *www.wolcott.com*

The 1871 House

(Map E–A3)

On the Upper East Side. This is special, a delightful NYC B&B. Only eight rooms or apartments at reasonable rents, some with terraces overlooking gardens. (There's no street number.)

⊠ *East 62nd Street,* ☎ *212 756 8823,* 💻 *www. 1891house.com*

Vanderbilt YMCA

(Map E–B3)

Despite the name both sexes can stop off here. This recently renovated hostel is in the heart of midtown east, has plenty of sports facilities and is close to the UN.

⊠ *224 East 47th St,* ☎ *212 756 9600,* 📠 *212 752 0210.*

Uptown

• ***LUXURY***

The Carlyle

(Map D–I3)

Notable older hotel in high Art Deco style, handy for the museums, Madison Avenue sale rooms and smart shops.

⊠ *35 East 76th Street,* ☎ *212 744 1600,* 📠 *717 4682,* *thecarlyle@rose woodhotels.com* 💻 *www.thecarlyle.com*

Lowell Hotel

(Map E–A3)

If you yearn for old-world comforts (even open fires in some rooms) and are willing to pay the price for high quality New York accommodation, this is a gem. It also has a very good restaurant.

Algonquin Round Table

Renowned for her smart quips ('you can lead a whore to culture but you cannot make her think'), **Dorothy Parker** was a queen among the wordsharps who met at the **Algonquin Hotel**, just over the road from the *New Yorker* offices. She and other wits held up a mirror to the times, and gave New York much of the image it preserves today as a centre of smart repartee, humorous verse and quick cracks. Alas, the Algonquin (on West 43rd Street) hasn't resounded with such hilarity for decades, but writers, agents and publishers still meet there and you can visit, have tea or a drink in its foyer, and enjoy its unique clubby atmosphere. You can even dine at the famous Round Table installed for the benefit of Dorothy Parker and her cohorts.

Bed and Breakfast

New York Bed and Breakfast does exist, and at a price you can stay with the genuine New Yorkers in their own homes. Try the following, but be sure to check ahead of arrival.

Bed and Breakfast Bureau, ✉ 330 West 42nd Street, ☎ 212 957 9786.

City Lights Bed and Breakfast Ltd, ✉ PO Box 20355, Cherokee Station, NYC, NY 10028, ☎ 212 737 8251.

New World Bed and Breakfast, ✉ 150 Fifth Avenue, no. 711, 10011, ☎ toll free: 800 443 3800 in USA and Canada, otherwise 675 5600.

✉ 28 East 63rd, ☎ 212 838 1400, 319 4230.

The Mark
(Map D–I4)
An elegant hotel on the Upper East Side close to the park and the Metropolitan Museum. Award-winning restaurant. Old-style European service and a club-like informal restaurant in the foyer.

✉ 25 East 77th Street, ☎ 212 744 4300, 744 2749, www.themarkhotel.com

• *BUDGET*

International Student Center
(Map D–H4)
You won't meet any Americans here – it's only open to foreigners, mostly students. It feels like old New York – a mansion on a leafy street – but there are dormitory rooms inside. It is close to Central Park.

✉ 38 West 88th St, ☎ 212 787 7706.

New York YHA International Hostel (Map D–I5)
This large hostel is well looked after, offers real bargain rates, varied services and has a lovely garden.

✉ 891 Amsterdam Avenue, ☎ 212 932 2300.

West Side YMCA
(Map E–A4)
Just off Central Park, this well-equipped (if a little severe in style) hostel has been very well renovated and offers bargain rooms with good sporting choices including an indoor running track.

✉ 5 West 63rd Street, ☎ 212 787 4400.

Hotel Beacon
(Map D–I5)
Top value for those who don't need to be central. Kitchen facilities, a good supermarket opposite.

✉ 2130 Broadway at 75th Street, ☎ 212 787 1100, 212 724 0839, info@beaconhotel.com

Downtown

• *LUXURY*

Millenium Hilton (Map E–H3)
Modern newly refurbished hotel by the WTC site, has great views and facilities for the business visitor.
✉ *55 Church Street,* ☎ *212 693 2001,* 📠 *571 2371,* 💻 *www.newyorkmillenium.hilton.com*

Ritz Carlton New York Battery Park (Map E–I4)
Luxurious waterfront Ritz Carlton, with superb harbour views.
✉ *2 West Street,* ☎ *212 344 0800,* 📠 *212 344 3804,* 💻 *www.ritzcarlton.com/hotels/new_york_battery_park*

• *MID-RANGE*

Chelsea Hotel (Map E–D4)
A rather bizarre hotel, its façade plastered with the names of the famous who have rested here, from Dylan Thomas to rock, punk and grunge stars.
✉ *222 West 23rd St,* ☎ *212 243 3700,* 📠 *675 5531.*

Gershwin Hotel (Map E–D3)
In a lively area near the new Sex Museum. Regular performances in the Living Room.
✉ *7 East 27th Street,* ☎ *212 545 8000,* 📠 *684 5546,* 💻 *www.gershwinhotel.com*

Holiday Inn Downtown (Map E–D4)
This is a conventional hotel in the Holiday Inn chain. Check low-price weekend rates through NYTAB.
✉ *138 Lafayette St, NYC 10013,* ☎ *212 966 8898,* 📧 *info@holidayinn-nyc.com* 💻 *www.holidayinn-nyc.com*

• *BUDGET*

Washington Square Hotel (Map E–F4)
Right on the famous Greenwich Village square, restaurant, fitness centre, best rooms have park view.
✉ *103 Waverly Place,* ☎ *212 777 9515,* 📠 *979 8373,* 💻 *www.washingtonsquarehotel.com*

Chelsea Center (Map E–D4)
Two low-priced hostels, simple accommodation, some dormitory style, and self-catering equipment.
✉ *313 West 29th St and* ✉ *East 12th St at 1st Avenue,* ☎ *212 643 0214.*

Airport

Mill River Manor (Map C–B2)
Increasingly people like staying out of the city and this is a fine choice only 20 minutes from the airport. Big rooms, local shops and restaurants, near Long Island Rail stop to NYC. Only 3 miles to fine sandy beaches.
✉ *173 Sunrise Highway, Rockville Center, Long Island,* ☎ *516 678 1300,* 📠 *516 678 5657,* 📧 *generalmanager@millrivermanor.com* 💻 *www.bestwestern.com/millrivermanor*

Above: *MacDonalds everywhere you look!*

EATING OUT
Cuisine

New York is one of those great gastronomic centres where the food range is enormous. It has some of the best food in the world and there are many very good restaurants, mainly in the Midtown area, as well as Chinatown and the Village. New York is a city of many styles and a place where **French food** really *is* French and not an imitation, as so often happens. Many French restaurateurs have moved to the city, particularly **Bretons**, and have opened upper-crust establishments, often luring leading French chefs to join their team.

There are also small and comfortable eateries where you can obtain a set-price meal that might make you feel you were in a lively French provincial city, if it weren't for the roar of the New York traffic just beyond the door.

Other than French and hearty native New York food (and there's nothing better, from the fresh seafood of Long Island to luscious Caesar salads, or steaks from the Midwest), there's a mouth-watering selection of different foods that you could sample for months and still not have gone through the whole menu. Add to these many small neighbourhood diners where a good breakfast can be very cheap – and a waitress will refill your cup at no extra charge. Children will love these straight-

Eating at the Station
American rail stations can be exotic: Art Deco palaces such as Los Angeles and Cincinnatti Ohio, and the truly grandiose **Grand Central** on East 42nd Street. Grand Central does not serve cross-country routes (as does Pennsylvania Station, now a series of underground vaults), but nevertheless it is a New York marvel. It now has a smart market for fish, meat and vegetables – good for self-caterers. Eat and drink here at unique places, or at chains like Starbucks. Try Michael Jordan's Steakhouse, or snack at Junior's Cheesecake, Cipriani Dolci, or enjoy cocktails at The Campbell Apartment.

forward American places which are popular with the locals and with Americans visiting out-of-town. You can either sit at the counter or at tables and eat delicious well-filled sandwiches or truly fat and mouth-watering hamburgers.

If you are on a budget, eating can be very cheap if you live on hot dogs or salads. Food and drink, particularly for light eating, has improved in the stations. Try the famous (but expensive) **Oyster Bar** at Grand Central (*see* also panel page 60). There are many food stalls and barrows on street corners, offering cheap snacks. For coffee and conversation, the new places are bookshops, where you'll find refreshment areas among the shelves, and these new arrivals stay open till late.

There's good news if you plan to eat around the Broadway theatre and cabaret area. The Theater District in the **West 40s** is undergoing a revival. **Eighth Avenue** is being cleaned up with a section devoted to restaurants. Newly revamped hotels in the area are smartening up too: the **Paramount** and the **Millennium** offer you a chance to eat right in the midst of things.

If there's one place you shouldn't miss it's **Chinatown** where there are a vast number of Oriental styles and

Ethnic Restaurants

Not so long ago it was not easy to find a good Indian restaurant in the city but the influx of Asians over the past 20 years has changed all that. They have been matched by Cubans, Koreans, Vietnamese, Japanese, Haitians, Thais, Russians and Central Americans, all bringing their own cuisines. You may need to seek your selection out (Russia, for example, is centred by the sea in an area now known as Little Odessa), but the choice of foods is amazing.

Below: *Food on roadside stands looks and smells good. But choose carefully.*

dishes. This once tight area, north of the Financial district, has expanded and is now very large. There is every type of restaurant available, from the cheap to the flamboyant, all mixed in with shops, markets and bars. It is hard to go wrong here, and prices are usually not that expensive. If it's a snack, dinner, or day-long dim sum you are after, you'll find it here. The city's Chinatown is a paradise for eaters, and highly recommended by local food critics too. Be warned: this is New York and writing about food and drink can be as arcane and folly ridden as some London or Paris reviews. Restaurants come and go quickly.

Next-door to Chinatown in **Little Italy** you can eat well, but do bear in mind that the food here is **Southern Italian**. Most immigrants came from Sicily and the south so it's solid pasta-and-heavy-tomato-sauce fare, and it's not cheap either. Look for seasonal celebrations in the city when all the food stalls are set up and you can try local snacks from Greek to Ukrainian or Cuban to Haitian, depending on the district. In New York the soul food (such as ribs, greens, corn bread, muffins and black-eyed beans) of the black community is worth trying too.

Table Talk

- **à la mode:** with ice cream.
- **bagel:** chewy bread roll often served with lox (smoked salmon) and cream cheese.
- **broiled:** grilled.
- **dim sum:** a parade of tiny steamed dumplings filled with meat, fish or vegetables.
- **eggs:** 'sunny side up' will be fried on one side only; 'over easy', fried quickly on both sides.
- **egg cream:** delicious concoction of iced milk, chocolate syrup and soda water.
- **hash browns:** fried potatoes with onion.
- **hero:** French bread sandwich.
- **jerk:** hot barbecued pork or chicken.
- **knish:** savoury dough filled with cheese or potato.
- **pretzel:** savoury bread twist sold on street corners.
- **check:** bill.

Below: *There are many fast-food joints on Central Station concourse.*

Drinks and Bars

Drinking in New York is a dream, whether your tipple is wine, beer, or those wondrous cocktails mixed with verve that really taste of liquor and

give an instant heady glow. You can have straight drinks in your hotel bar, romantic cocktails in lofty settings overlooking Manhattan, or dip into one of the neighbourhood bars where half the clientele will be watching a game on the ubiquitous TV. Irish bars abound, especially along Second and Third Avenues, and probably the most atmospheric one of all is McSorley's in the Village, which is a classic hangout. Many of the others offer good beer, local and imported, as well as live music and jazz.

Above: *New York diners are popular with locals and the food is usually good.*

Another marvellous thing about New York City is that whatever atmosphere you are looking for in a bar, you will be able to find it somewhere or other. Bars vary: from singles to sophisticated, arty to odd, theatrical caves or thumping musical dives, gregarious to gay. The selection is enormous and it is changing all the time. The opening hours in some of these establishments can go on forever: often, closing time merely means the doors shut in the early morning hours between 04:00 and 06:00 in order for them to be able to clean up the joint. As a result many of the bars don't get going until very late at night, especially at weekends. If this is your scene you could be in heaven.

Wine
Although you can choose from a wide range of the world's best in New York, you may want to sample a few American wines. Many chefs will gladly introduce you to the 'local' wines and a surprise are the fast evolving New York State wines from the Finger Lakes. Wine producers are proliferating and they aren't all in sunny California: some good bottles (particularly white) are also emerging from Washington State.

Cosmopolitan Cuisine

Ducks hang everywhere in Chinese restaurants in Lower Manhattan, especially in old Chinatown along Mott and Mulberry Streets. But what's this? Once a separate neighbourhood, Little Italy has merged into Chinatown and now the cluttered sidewalks offer Neapolitan pizza, Sicilian sauces and Milanese rice dishes as well as Chinese noodles and dumplings. Along a renewed Broadway and the Bowery, many other places lure the nose with their food smells. Low-priced snack bars and eateries of all kinds, from American to Jewish, are now joined by new offerings from Caribbean and Asian arrivals.

Restaurants

The range of restaurants and eateries in this city is enormous. From local bakeries and hot dog stands where you can nibble on snacks as you sightsee, to chic cafés and department store restaurants, right up to the top-of-the-range-eateries, there is an awe-inspiring choice. Even the cheap food places are often very good. There are many specialist places to choose from, such as Jewish dairy cafés and a delectable parade of vegetarian restaurants.

There are also quite a number of Indian places now but it seems that every country in the world is represented in this very food-conscious city with its parade of particular cuisines from Australia to Zambia.

Look out for local fairs and celebrations: some of these, such as Little Italy's festival, are well known, but look out for others too. Festivals are a lively time when whole neighbourhoods turn out to parade and dance in the streets. During Restaurant Week, held in the last week in June, hundreds of establishments offer taster portions and special prix-fixe meals.

Also, don't miss the dozens of Chinese restaurants around Mulberry Street. Ask for the latest recommendation in a variety of cuisines from the humblest Cantonese to Pekingese and the spicy Szechwan.

Foodies can go mad at the very thought of New York's incredible range of restaurants, and if you have money to spend, there are some of the leading restaurants in the world to try. Almost all good establishments will take credit cards, and New York is a city where hotel restaurants are often of a high standard too.

Midtown

• *LUXURY*

La Côte Basque

A very smart restaurant serving classic French food. Famous for its evocative murals and a unique style all of its own.

✉ *60 West 55th Street,*
☎ *212 688 6525.*

The Four Seasons

This is one of the sights of foodie New York, but it's not only famous as a temple to gastronomes, it is very grand and social. It's the place to try if you want to see smart New York at table.

✉ *99 East 52nd Street,*
☎ *212 754 9494.*

The Rainbow Room

Now owned by Cipriani, this is a prime place to dine and dance, but it's expensive. Still, with those views from the 65th floor you should lose your head a bit. There's a nightclub too, and if you're not so hungry try the Rainbow Promenade situated nearby.

✉ *230 Rockefeller Plaza,*
☎ *212 632 5000.*

• *MID-RANGE*

La Cité

This restaurant is large and rambling and great for good straightforward food (it serves delicious hamburgers) and big refreshing drinks.

✉ *120 West 51st Street,* ☎ *212 956 7100,* 🖳 www.citerestaurant.com

Pierre au Tunnel

This restaurant is close to the ever-busy tunnel across to

Above: *Empire Diner in Manhattan.*

Sunshine

Like most Americans New Yorkers like new ideas. The latest is concerned with not cutting out the sun. Who wants to eat on a terrace in shadow? So-called 'air rights' here resulted in increasing lack of natural daylight at street level due to large overshadowing buildings, as low-rise places sold air rights. The answer? They want huge mirrors attuned to sunlight to beam down precious light from the skyscrapers stealing it. This should make eating out a brighter experience!

West Side Eating

Eating out poses no problems here, with a host of restaurants of all ethnic persuasions. But perhaps best of all is the array of shops offering tantalizing snacks and takeaway foods: from imported coffees to cakes there's everything here. Many offer Jewish specialities. The famous **Zabar's** has many kinds of bread, as well as delicatessen items, and it's usually crowded with people buying their favourite, be it hard dark rye or zesty poppy seed rolls.

Queens. The unusual thing about New York is the number of authentic French restaurants it has, and this one is just like an old bistro.

✉ 250 East 47th Street,
☎ 212 575 1220.

The Palm

If you feel like a steak then this crazy, but fun restaurant is just the place for you. In addition to a good steak there is lobster and that very New York dish, Clams Casino. The place is busy and lively.

✉ 837 Second Avenue, and there are other branches at 840 Second Avenue and at 250 W 50th,
☎ 212 687 2953.

Time

Offers basic foods, from pizzas to tapas, as well as special dishes. Friendly and crowded, with a nice bar area.

✉ at Lafayette Place,
☎ 212 533 7000, or
✉ 2330 Broadway at 8th Street.

Moto

This may be the best Japanese restaurant in town. Smallish menu, very friendly, good value. It is open evenings only, closed on Mondays.

✉ 328 West 45th Street,
☎ 212 459 9393.

• *BUDGET*

La Fondue

If cheese is a passion, try this for the all-in-one experience. They also do beef, fish and seafood, so you don't just have to eat cheese. Afterwards try the chocolate fondue. Low-price, so no credit cards.

Below: *Zabar's isn't just a famed Jewish delicatessen and bakery. It's a New York institution.*

✉ *43 West 55th Street,* ☎ *212 581 0820.*

Planet Hollywood

This is the in place for kids; there is so much going on as they eat that the food hardly matters. It is very popular, so you can expect to wait.

✉ *1540 Broadway,* ☎ *212 333 7827.*

Carmine's

A noisy, friendly, family place with a typically New York-Italian atmosphere. It is open late; serves home-style food.

✉ *200 West 44th Street,* ☎ *212 221 3800, with a branch uptown at* ✉ *2450 Broadway at 90th Street.*

Whaler Bar

American-style snacks and drinks are served before a big roaring fire in this lofty place. Entertainment is also provided. This bar is very popular with the locals.

✉ *in the Jolly Hotel Madison Towers at 22 East 38th Street,* ☎ *212 685 3700.*

Uptown

• ***Mid-range***

Elaine's

This is the sort of personality cult place that only happens in big cities. It is so popular that the food, which is eclectic, doesn't matter.

✉ *1703 Second Avenue,* ☎ *212 534 8103.*

Primavera

This quietly elegant place is popular with the locals. Friendly, concerned Italian service.

✉ *1578 First Avenue,* ☎ *212 861 8608,* 💻 *www.primavera.com*

Mark's

A charming in-hotel restaurant off the foyer, offering French-American food all day long in an intimate setting.

✉ *25 East 77th Street,* ☎ *212 879 1864,*

American Chefs

There are many fine restaurants on the East Side. Don't assume that when you see the label 'American' on a food description that it means hamburger, fries and coleslaw. Not any more. In many restaurants new chefs are creating wonderful, fresh ideas in US cooking. You may need to go to a pricey place to taste what the new generation is up to but it'll be worth it.

East Side Wining and Dining

There's lots of choice for eating and drinking in the East Village, and many unusual places to choose from. It's noted for old-style bars such as McSorley's Old Ale House on East 7th Street, which claims to be the oldest in the country. Ethnic food abounds. There's still an Italian presence, with pastry shops north of 10th Street, and Polish restaurants. The strong Ukrainian flavour is reinforced by the restaurants as well as the annual festival which is held in May along East 7th Street, around the Ukrainian Church of St George. On East Sixth Street is another enclave of Indian settlers where you will find many enticing restaurants.

🖳 *www.themark hotel.com*

• ***BUDGET***

American Trash

As you'd suspect from the name, this eatery is for the kids and there's usually a queue to get in.

✉ *1471 First Avenue,* ☎ *212 988 9008.*

Bistro du Nord

You'll find this great little French restaurant at East 93rd Street before you reach Spanish Harlem. It has a warm, welcoming atmosphere, and reasonably priced French food.

✉ *1312 Madison Avenue,* ☎ *212 289 0997.*

Downtown

• ***MID-RANGE***

Katz's Delicatessen Inc

This deli caters mostly for older people (and younger ones too!) who enjoy traditional kosher food.

✉ *205 East Houston,* ☎ *212 254 2246,* 🖳 *www.katzdel.com*

Cowgirl

Lively Southwestern atmosphere and cooking. A new favourite.

✉ *519 Hudson Street at 10th,* ☎ *212 633 1133.*

• ***BUDGET***

Koodo Sushi

This establishment is located in a plain space beneath the Seaport Suites, but makes good sushi – try a take-out to eat on Pier 16 or 17.

✉ *129 Front Street,* ☎ *212 425 2890.*

Café Reggio

Everything you expect of a village café – where unusual people gather for snacks.

✉ *119 MacDougal Street,* ☎ *212 475 9557.*

If Café Reggio is crowded, **Café Dante** is equally atmospheric.

✉ *79 MacDougal,* ☎ *212 982 5275.*

Dean and Deluca Café

Spin-off from the renowned groceries (there's a big one at the roadway corner) in SoHo. This is a good place to enjoy a snack or have coffee.

✉ *121 Prince Street,* ☎ *212 254 8776.*

Fedora's

This restaurant has been a village landmark for more than 50 years. Serving big drinks and cheap eats, it's a bit tatty, but charming Fedora is still hostess here. (No credit cards.)

✉ *239 West 4th Street,* ☎ *212 242 9691.*

Queens

Though this borough once had little to commend itself for visitors, it's now much livelier – and so is the food. Along the busy avenue in Central Queens beside the elevated subway line are neighbourhood bars and good eateries from Indian to Oriental, often at bargain rates. Walk along and check the menus for bargain meals.

• ***LUXURY***
Water's Edge
A smart place that takes advantage of Manhattan views. This seafood restaurant is on the city edge of Long Island in Queens, and formal. Complimentary water shuttle from Manhattan
✉ *44th Drive, Long Island City,*
☎ *718 482 0033.*

• ***BUDGET***
Pastrami King
New Yorkers get sentimental about where to get good salt beef, or pastrami, and this is a real 'deli'.
✉ *124-24 Queens Boulevard,*
☎ *718 263 1717.*

Brooklyn

• ***LUXURY***
River Café
Just to show that not all of the expensive places are situated in Manhattan itself, this smart spot cashes in on the view from Brooklyn – it is located near the famous landmark Brooklyn Bridge where the one-time barge is moored.
✉ *1 Water Street, Brooklyn Heights,*
☎ *718 522 5200,*
🖳 *www.theriver cafe.com*

• ***MID-RANGE***
Henry's End
Good value to be found here, and unusual cuisine – such as kangaroo and elk.
✉ *44 Henry Street, Brooklyn,*
☎ *718 834 1776.*

Odessa
So you want to try the new Russia? Come to Brighton Beach and try the parade of dishes and vodka, and dancing too.
✉ *1113 Brighton Beach Avenue,*
☎ *718 648 6044.*

Places to Eat
Although some NYC restaurants claim star status and charge accordingly, you can eat very well in many ordinary places. Plain American cooking is good – from soups to thick, well-stuffed sandwiches. Hamburgers and steaks are prime here, salads well mixed and dressed, pies hearty and piled with fillings. And American cocktails tend to be generously laced, stylishly presented. Coffee is good and you should not miss a New York breakfast.

Below: *A member of the Hard Rock chain. These eateries are known for their rock and roll memorabilia.*

Right: *The St Patrick's Day Parade, when the Irish community in New York honour their paton saint, is a spectacle in green.*

ENTERTAINMENT
The Arts

New York as a place just to eat, shop and indulge yourself wouldn't bring in many tourists, and with no arts the city would be a poor place. This is one of the liveliest and most creative places on the planet. Without **Broadway**, without magnificent museums, libraries and galleries, without book and record shops, without buzzing and intriguing centres of painting, sculpture and writing, without that incredible architecture, there would indeed be very few reasons to come here. It's all going on non-stop in such vital centres as Midtown, Greenwich Village, SoHo, TriBeCa and the Upper West Side, with the added attraction of their parades of unusual characters.

Festivals

- **Chinatown's New Year** is celebrated in late January– early February.
- In **Little Italy** the lights go up for the **San Gennaro** festival in September. On this Saint's day, his shrine and relics are paraded through the streets. There's music, dancing, Italian food and drink as well as stalls and fairground side shows.
- The settlement on East 7th Street, located around the church of St George, celebrates its **Ukrainian** roots during May.
- Indian special events are many and the residents of **Little India** on East 6th Street mark such times as **Diwali** with fireworks and festivities.

Festivals and Parades

There's hardly a week that goes by without some form of parade or celebration and these events tend to be big, gregarious and great fun.

The **Columbus Day Parade** draws huge crowds. Whole areas may be transformed,

whether for local festivals or big events. On **St Patrick's Day**, Fifth Avenue and even the flowers in their stands are coloured green, and the parade is received by dignitaries on the steps of St Patrick's Cathedral. The locals of the East Village celebrate the **Ukrainian Festival** in May. The most famous is **San Gennaro's** in Little Italy, where you can nosh on Italian food as you parade under festive lights; and newly established Indian settlements (there are several 'Little Indias') offer Hindu celebrations such as **Diwali**. This is a major Hindu religious festival honouring the goddess of Wealth. It is characterized by feasting, presents and the lighting of lamps.

Many of these events are ethnic, yet wherever you come from, you will feel welcome. For dates and information on such events the Convention and Visitors' Bureau (*see* page 84) has listings.

The Big Parade

Every November a big event hits New York as well as TV screens across the entire country. It's the renowned **Macy's Thanksgiving Day Parade** when the store (*see* page 52) sponsors a huge procession of decorated floats, specially shaped helium balloons, crowds of costumed extras including cartoon characters, dancing and drumming bands and in the last float who do you think? Jolly old Santa Claus with his reindeer of course, to remind us all that at heart it's still a commercial event.

Theatre

To find out what's on in **Broadway**, check newspapers and weekly arts guides. There are always the big musical and dramatic play hits, and these can be expensive, but there is a range of ticket prices and some bargains. The top talent performs on Broadway, from the big box office stars to supporting actors, dancers, singers, designers and also directors. Performances usually start on Tuesday and carry on to Sunday. Be sure to book.

Below: *Just one of several streets in the Theatre District.*

Carnegie Hall
⊠ 57th Street at 7th Avenue, 10019
☎ 212 247 7800

Lincoln Center
⊠ 70 Lincoln Center Plaza, Columbus Ave and 62nd, 10023
☎ 212 875 5000
💻 www.lincoln center.org
Metropolitan Opera
☎ 212 362 6000
💻 www.metopera.org

Madison Square Garden
See panel, page 41

Shea Stadium
See panel, page 41

Meadowlands
⊠ East Rutherford NJ Stadium, NJ 07073
☎ 201 935 8222

Apollo Theater
⊠ 253 125th at 7th Avenue
☎ 212 531 5300
💻 www.apollo theatre.com

The same goes for the vibrant movement known as **Off-Broadway**, which has a range of theatres all over Midtown and in the East and West Village. Often these smaller houses will have unusual, provocative plays with top artists and some of them, such as the lively **Manhattan Project**, often bring new shows to Broadway and beyond.

Music and Dance

New York is a music town and there is much of it here, from symphony concerts to recitals, band events and pop concerts. In summer, the parks have open-air concerts which are free and very popular. World-renowned **Carnegie Hall** is now the home of the NY Philharmonic, **Lincoln Center** offers packed programmes and don't neglect the **Juilliard School** for small events.

A revered concert hall in high Victorian style, Carnegie Hall is a place artists are proud to play in. It's over a century old, yet its acoustics are rated so highly that the New York Philharmonic is relocating here. After a concert you may catch a glimpse of the stars at nearby restaurants and bars.

For major pop concerts, the big venues like **Madison Square Garden, Shea Stadium** and **Meadowlands** can cater for the crowds. For major black stars (and minor ones on Wednesday Amateur Night), the new-look **Apollo Theater** is back in business. It features top entertainers per-

Carnegie Hall **(above)** *and Lincoln Center* **(opposite)** *are two of New York's major concert venues.*

forming the blues, gospel and jazz. Other live music venues include **Brooklyn Academy** and **Avery Fisher Hall** for the New York Philharmonic. Check the freesheets or the *New York Times* for the current concert schedules. For an intimate musical evening check what's on at **Alice Tully Hall**.

The New York City Ballet is resident dance company at the **State Theater**. Like the Met, this theatre is used by visiting companies when the principal occupant is touring or on leave. This ballet company continues to flourish in the style of George Balanchine, who founded it; an evening here can be very exciting.

As dance is such a big interest in New York there is much activity, from classical to modern and experimental. See alternative publications or the *Village Voice*.

Opera

The **Lincoln Center** (*see* page 31) is synonymous with opera and dance. One of the few companies to pursue an expansive repertory system is the **Metropolitan Opera**, with a different work on every night except Sundays. American Ballet Theatre is the resident company and there are dance events when the opera season is not in progress.

Brooklyn Academy of Music
⊠ 30 Lafayette St, Brooklyn 11217
☎ 718 636 4100
🖳 www.bam.org

Avery Fisher Hall
⊠ 10 Lincoln Centre
☎ 212 875 5656
🖳 www.newyorkphilharmonic.org

Alice Tully Hall
⊠ 70 Lincoln Center Plaza
☎ 212 875 5788
🖳 www.chambermusicsociety.org

NY State Theater
☎ 212 870 5570
🖳 www.nycopera.com
www.lincolncenter.org

Above: *Radio City Music Hall is a big attraction, and a monument to the Art Deco style.*

Cabaret

Greenwich Village saw the blossoming of a few of the first small theatres away from Broadway. Here Off-Broadway is very well represented, and so is Off-Off-Broadway, with cheaper spaces in the less wholesome parts. Some of these theatres present quite surprising shows, although it's difficult to shock the neighbours. But this is the place for lively cafés and cabaret entertainment, and you can find plenty of small stages with stand-up comics, musicians and singers trying out their act.

Horse Racing

New Yorkers love 'a flutter' (they love to bet), and their tastes are well catered for, with several tracks close to the city reachable on public transport. You can catch where there's horse racing on local radio stations. Popular are **Aqueduct**, out near Kennedy Airport, with a season from Oct–May, and **Belmont Park** with thoroughbred flat racing May–Jul and Sep–Oct. The track at **Meadowlands** in East Rutherford, New Jersey, also has that unusual sport of trotting from Jan–Aug and is open Mon–Sat.

Gambling

Unusually New York City has no casinos, unlike major towns in Europe where they are popular and have a smart aspect. Casinos in North America are often in former reservations, owned by Native Americans. Many Americans cross the border to gamble In nearby Canada: converted or new buildings are much more proletariat with hordes of machines beside traditional card and roulette tables. However, there are casinos in New Jersey, and at several NYC race tracks betting is permitted (*see* panel).

Nightlife

There's plenty of activity after dark in the city's many clubs and cabarets. They range from rough and raunchy to very smart and expensive, so there's a wide choice. **Bars** can be found all over; they are often very local

and friendly, with generous drinks and not too expensive. Most **nightclubs** and cabarets are in central Manhattan around the redeveloped and safe Times Square, or based in the smart streets and hotels on the East Side. Increasingly some are in the newly developed areas in the South and West of Lower Manhattan's one-time working and meat market areas. Local ones in Brooklyn, the Bronx and Queens are much lower key and cheaper, yet they can be great fun. Expect to pay an entry fee and high prices for cocktails and eats at the smart places, but then the entertainment is free once you are ensconced in your comfortable chairs, or at the bar. **Shows** can be very good indeed, from tall leggy girls in wisps of costume to hot musical events with top singers, and you can even find **satirical revue**, which is most likely to be in cellars in Greenwich Village.

Of course there are many big **clubs** just dedicated to dancing, music coming from latest hits which often feature the hottest bands and lots of flamboyant exhibitionism. Clubs range from those with all-young crowds to mega-gay events. Bars here close very late, and so do clubs, often not heating up until midnight is past. **Restaurants** can be vibrant at night too, sometimes with entertainment, and the classic Rainbow Room and other high-in-the-air places are very popular. If you are uncertain which joint may be just right for you, read the local listings or ask your hotel concierge.

Fashionable Nightlife

Fashions swing wildly among the clubs, especially for the young, the wealthy and the trendy. One that's 'in' one month may well be 'out' in a year or less. If you want to be in with the current crowd you will need to ask around. People dress to kill and show off. There's usually a lot of star-spotting too, for famous faces can often be seen. Stars know that New York's night scene is the hottest, smartest and – sometimes – the wildest one around.

Below: *The Playpen in 42nd Street is just one of New York's night spots.*

Above: *The Blue Note Jazz Club is a popular venue and features leading jazz musicians.*

Something for Everyone
Entertainment offered in nightclubs and bars is designed for a wide public. You can get jazz, the latest hits, piano music, blues, or karaoke. There's live comedy at Comic Strip Live, the World Famous Laugh Factory and an annual comedy month in October at 40 locations. Many of the clubs have disabled facilities too. Don't want to stray too far? Check the big hotels for glossy cabarets or supper clubs.
For updated nightclub information check
🖳 www.newyears.com
☎ 212 843v2400.

Nightclubs, Bars and Discos

Atrium Lounge
Start with cocktails in the dramatic lofty setting of the Marriott Marquis atrium. Also try its Broadway Lounge with views of Times Square from the 8th floor.
⊠ 45th and Broadway, ☎ 212 398 1900 (Atrium), 212 704 8900 (Broadway Lounge).

Blue Bar
In the Algonquin Hotel, this popular pub-like bar is crowded at cocktail time.
⊠ 59 West 44th,
☎ 212 840 6800,
🖳 www.algonquinhotel.com

Blue Note
Village jazz club with leading artists, two shows nightly, dinner.
⊠ 131 West 3rd St,
☎ 212 475 8592,
🖳 www.bluenotejazz.com

Branch
A hot spot club, newest DJ's, sunken dance floor, Spanish tapas snacks.
⊠ 226 East 54th St,
☎ 212 688 5577,
🖳 www.branchny.com
🕒 Closed Sun–Wed.

Bridges Bar
This hotel lounge offers a wide range of New York's famous gin or vodka martinis.
⊠ Hilton NY, 54th at 6th Avenue,
☎ 212 586 7000,
🖳 www.newyorktowers.hilton.com

Bubble Lounge
Down in the newly vibrant Tribeca, this bar offers cocktails in a deluxe setting.
⊠ 228 West Broadway, ☎ 212 431 3433,
🖳 www.bubblelounge.com

Café Carlyle
Leading entertainers

are in cabaret at this very chic supper club.
✉ *The Carlyle, 35 East 76th,* ☎ *212 744 1600,* 💻 *www.thecarlyle.com* 🕒 *Closed Sun.*

Cellar Bar
Fashionable central Manhattan cocktail spot with leading DJ's.
✉ *Bryant Park Hotel, 40 West 40th,* ☎ *212 869 0100,* 💻 *www.bryantparkhotel.com* 🕒 *Closed Sun.*

Cherry
All-night spot for the young and glam set in lively red leather room.
✉ *120 East 39th St,* ☎ *212 519 8508,* 💻 *www.mocbars.com*

Comic Strip Live
Famed comedy club where the acts are the top comedians.
✉ *1568 2nd Ave at 81st,* ☎ *212 861 9386,* 💻 *www.comicstriplive.com*

Copacabana
Dance floors, top DJ's and bands. A classic.
✉ *560 W 34th,* ☎ *212 239 2672,* 💻 *www.thecopacabana.com* 🕒 *Open till 05:00.*

Gotham Comedy Club
Lively new comedy acts, buzzy atmosphere. American eats.
✉ *34 West 22nd St,* ☎ *212 367 9000,* 💻 *www.gothamcomedyclub.com*

Hudson's Sports Bar & Grill Satellite
Here you can enjoy sports coverage on dozens of monitors.
✉ *Sheraton New York Hotel Towers, at West 52nd St,* ☎ *212 581 1000,* 💻 *www.sheraton.com*

Lenox Lounge
Jazz club in Harlem, great history of top names, with soul food and live jazz.
✉ *288 Lenox Ave at 125th St.* ☎ *212 427 0253.*

Manahatta
In the East Village, this cocktail bar offers DJ music and tapas.
✉ *316 Bowery,* ☎ *212 253 8644,* 💻 *www.manahatta.us* 🕒 *Closed Sun.*

Show Nightclub
Paris and Pigalle are the triggers here. This nightclub is centrally located.
✉ *6th Ave and Broadway at 135 West 41st,* ☎ *212 278 0988,* 💻 *www.shownightclub.com*

13
A classic New York bar and club, this lively place is near Union Square.
✉ *35 E 13th St,* ☎ *212 979 6677,* 💻 *www.bar13.com*

Underbar
A sexy underground cocktail hangout for the adventurous fun seeker. Private booths.
✉ *201 Park Ave South,* ☎ *212 358 1560,* 💻 *www.mocbars.com*

The Whiskey
Smart, with screening room and crazy liquid-gel dance space.
✉ *1567 Broadway,* ☎ *212 930 7444,* 💻 *www.mocbars.com*

Above: *Where the wealthy play – yachts in the Sound off Long Island.*

EXCURSIONS

Inland and also along the Eastern Seaboard there are many interesting places that will make an ideal day or half day out, be it a country tour, a trip to a beach, a theme park, or an historic town. There are many choices for days out by coach, self-drive car or train beyond the reach of local transport, into New York State, up into Connecticut or across into New Jersey. All three states have surprising countryside and tourist attractions of their own. There is a variety of things to do beyond the borders of the city and a wide range of places to visit, all within a short distance. The various tourist boards will happily assist you. Be sure to ask about bargain day-out fares as well as the special offers on coaches.

Long Island Country

Inland Long Island is often overlooked, yet its country pleasures are delightful. Rural roads, sea views, little restaurants offering local seafood such as the delicious tiny Bay Scallops. Try them broiled in butter. Small farms grow potatoes, corn and vegetables; there are lots of roadside stands in season to sell you fresh produce for picnics. You'll find plenty of quiet places for alfresco meals too. And note Woodbury Common for great bargains, just an hour from New York City.

Long Island

New York is a marvellous place for a holiday but don't forget that the city, with its complex web of transport, both local and long distance, is also perfect as a base for the discovery of other cities, out-of-town sites and local centres of attraction.

Long Island is a case in point. This huge piece of land, some 120 miles (193km) long, parallels Connecticut's coast and extends into the Atlantic. It is essentially rural once you leave the New York suburbs. Trains depart from **Pennsylvania Station** (also known as Penn Station) but can be crowded at certain times of the day because they serve so many commuters.

Long Island
Location: Map C–C1
Distance from New York City: Long Island commences just across the East River from Manhattan.

Long Island Railroad
☎ 718 217 5477 (MTA Long Island Railroad)
☎ 718 217 5477 (MTA Long Island Bus)

You'll discover an undulating landscape that becomes ever more countrified as you go further northeast, with small settlements and neat farms. Trains are slow and the carriages are hardly modern, yet you get the best view this way: if you drive yourself in a hire-car you may find it hard to navigate on the elevated highways. Many Long Island resorts are accessed by jitney buses from New York City.

The **Long Island Railroad** will give you a real taste of the island, from pastures to open sea. Especially popular in summer, it will also take you to a number of resorts along the east coast as well as commuter suburbs. There are beaches all around the island, but those facing the open sea are peerless wide stretches of white sand. Lapped by the Atlantic, with long, cleansing rollers, the shore is a perfect destination even out of season, but wonderful on a hot summer day. At weekends, though, parks and beaches may be very crowded with New Yorkers bent on escaping the city heat. It's a good idea to take a picnic and to use the barbecue facilities offered in state parks. There are many of these facilities and they are free.

The train stops at ferry points for the thin spit of sandy land known as **Fire Island**, a very popular destination in summer, dotted with resorts for every taste. The 40-odd summer settlements are connected by walkways and cater for families, singles and gay people. Fire Island is a long sandbar protecting the east

Below: *Fire Island is a line of sand protecting Long Island from the Atlantic. There are superb beaches here.*

The NYCard and Map
Of great use to visitors is a discount card and city map, called the NYCard. It saves on museums, attractions and accommodation. In a neat pocket-sized packet, the map is one of the best. NY Travel Advisory Bureau mails it in their visitor kit worldwide. Order through their website: www.nytab.com

coast of the island, home to small parks and a chain of seaside resorts, and the beaches are wide and clean.

About two hours along the coast are the resorts known as **The Hamptons** – the neat little towns of Westhampton, South and Easthampton, the latter pair wildly chic in summer, expensive and filled with New Yorkers on vacation. It's as if the entire Upper East Side had flown out like exotic birds to perch here in cool summer cottages.

You can continue further to the remote end of Long Island and **Amagansett**, which is where the rich and the less flamboyant have summer houses to get away from it all. The sands are wide, the sky and sea views huge and the beaches are often deserted. If you want an experience of peace then it is advisable to come out of season.

New Jersey and Pennsylvania

To the west is New Jersey. From the bluffs of the Hudson River just across the George Washington Bridge you get fine views of Manhattan from the Palisade's Parkway. **Newark**, much improved, has a good museum and office buildings rise over Mulberry Fishmarket.

An hour's train journey will take you to **Princeton**, an Ivy League university. The elegant small university town's campus is all in approved stone Gothic style. Friendly and photogenic, there are pretty white-fenced streets and clapboard houses.

Even the rich repository of arts and architecture and the city of Brotherly Love, **Philadelphia**, in

Below: *Philadelphia is just a bus ride, or a ninety-minute train journey, away from New York City.*

Left: *Colourful Victorian houses in Cape May.*

the state of Pennsylvania, is only a 90-minute bus journey away.

Ugly **Hoboken**, **Jersey City** and **Elizabeth** may be, with their heavy industry and rundown houses, but they are not typical. Beyond them you will find some pretty countryside and, in the west, some smart 'hunting country'.

In the far west is the lovely **Delaware Water Gap** along the wide river valley – drive and enjoy the small settlements and wonderful old inns on the Delaware banks, and New Jersey towns like **Flemington** and **Lambertville**. Here you can cross into Pennsylvania and the town of **New Hope**, the centre for the beautifully rustic Bucks County.

The sea coast of New Jersey, with wild country and wonderful extensive beaches, is a world away from Long Island, although in its long sweep from New York's harbour to the lonely country of **Cape May**, it has attractive seaside communities. The major one gained immense favour in the early part of the 20th century as a getaway place for New Yorkers. This is **Atlantic City**, with its famous attractions and sandy beaches.

Atlantic City reached a high-water mark in the 1920s (evoked in the musical *42nd Street*), but since then has declined in

Indian Connections

An Indian place name (Quinnehtuqut) was the original name of the river cutting through the state of Connecticut. There are many other examples of Indian place names in the state, some attached to scenic attractions, such as the Shepaug River Gorge, Lake Waramaug and the Housatonic River. The name Washington isn't Indian of course, but in the town is a collection of Indian archaeology and a replica of a Native American village.

The Port Authority Bus Terminal

A very important link for coach and bus travel, the terminal is a 24-hour operation. You can cross America from here – or take coaches to the three city airports. Clean, well-ordered and safe, it has good cafés and bars.

Above: *The main promenade at Atlantic City.*

fashion, although it continues to host major meetings and the occasional party conference. The city still has the usual seaside attractions plus a casino and some lures: the famous wooden boardwalk that runs along the promenade above the beach was the place to be seen 75 years ago. The town has had to revamp itself, but its old hotels have character and charm.

Connecticut

North from New York is **New England**. This area of six states has much to offer and two of them are within easy reach of New York. The most southerly is Connecticut.

You can get to **New Haven** by bus or train. A comfortable town first laid out in the 17th century, New Haven has fine museums and three early churches at its centre. It is also the home of **Yale**, another member of the Ivy League club, and guided tours leave from Phelps Gate. You could visit the state capital, **Hartford**, with its handsome state capitol building and connections with 19th-century novelists Mark Twain and Harriet Beecher-Stowe. You can even go as far as Providence to discover the state of **Rhode Island** and **Newport** with its palatial summer houses built for the New York rich with French chateaus in mind. These destinations would be served better with a night's stopover to avoid having a frustratingly short stay.

Connecticut has a string of beaches. If you can get as far as **Mystic** you'll discover an old

Yale

Aside from Princeton, for a really different day you can visit the university town of Yale. Take the train from Grand Central up to New Haven in Connecticut. This old town (with a famous theatre, the Long Wharf) spreads round the Yale campus which is large and handsome, with baronial buildings, galleries and open spaces. Major university football games are a draw – but make sure you have tickets if you want to attend.

whaling station and a maritime museum where craftsmen display old sea-going skills. Nearby **New London** is a lively place that has associations with the writer Eugene O'Neill.

Connecticut is also very rural once you have crossed its southern commuter belt. It has small farms and old-style towns and villages. Some are typically New England with quite a different character in its residents. If you only have time for one or two then consider **Litchfield** or **Wethersfield**, both with a wealth of Colonial houses.

Lower New York State

New York is a huge state with many attractions, but such lures as **Lake Champlain**, the **Finger Lakes**, **Rochester** and the **Ontario shore** are too far for day trips. The southern part of the state has much to offer, though, and it's charmingly low-key and agreeable.

A drive along the **Hudson River Valley** from New York has many pleasures and a host of small state and historic parks to visit. Stop at **West Point Military Academy**, for its museum and visitor centre, or scan the views from **Bear Mountain**. Stately homes are the **Vanderbilt Mansion**, the **Mills Mansion** and **Hyde Park**, the Springwood estate of Franklin D Roosevelt. These beautiful homes are to be found in the neighbourhood of **Poughkeepsie**, once the state capital. At the present state capital of **Albany** there's much to take in too. Another beautifully rural drive can be followed through the **Catskill Mountains**, where Washington Irving's fictional character Rip van Winkle fell asleep.

New Jersey Tourist Office
🖳 www.state.nj.us

Pennsylvania Tourist Office
🖳 www.state.pa.us

Connecticut Tourist Office
🖳 www.tourism.state.ct.us

Tourist Office of New York State
In the USA:
🖳 www.iloveny.com
☎ 1 800 iloveny

In Europe:
✉ NY State Division of Tourism, 3 Lonsdale Road, NW6 6RA, London
☎ 20 7629 6891 (from outside the UK)
🖰 iloveny@nyseurope.com

Below: *The Catskill Mountains, setting for the story of Rip van Winkle.*

Above: *A confusing array of street signs adorn poles on the city's street corners.*

Public Holidays
January 1 • New Year's Day
January 15 • Martin Luther King Day
3rd Monday in May • Presidents' Day
Last Monday in May • Memorial Day
July 4 • Independence Day
1st Monday in September • Labour Day
November 11 • Veterans Day
4th Thursday in November • Thanksgiving Day
December 25 • Christmas Day

Tourist Information

As cutbacks cause the closure of government agencies, the private sector is taking over tourist information. The New York Travel Advisory Bureau's visitor kit (*see* panel page 87) offers maps, discount and information; obtainable in the UK, ☎ 0906 11 22 668. Calls cost about £4, covering shipping of two kits by Global Priority Mail. Try the **New York Convention and Visitors Bureau**, ✉ 810 Seventh Avenue, NY 10019, ☎ 212 484 1222, 📠 245 5943, 💻 www.nytab.com (for information, not personal visits). In some countries the State of New York may be represented in its own right.

Entry Requirements

You will need a valid passport to enter the United States, and check new regulations in force after 9/11. You may need a visa so ask at the visa division of your local US Embassy or consulate. Fingerprints are taken and there is a plan to make iris (eye) records. Non US residents fill in two forms on arrival and queues form before booths as each entrant is interviewed at the entry point, which can take time.

Customs

Immigration and custom formalities at most airports are now swift and efficient. At some airports sniffer dogs are used to check baggage and they will also indicate if you are carrying fresh fruit, vegetable, dairy or meat products. Check beforehand what is not allowed for importation. There

are certain duty-free allowances to every visitor and US resident so find out what these are before you buy.

Health Requirements

No inoculation certificates are needed, unless you have recently been in an area with an epidemic of yellow fever, cholera, or other contagious sickness. You may be interviewed if you have recently visited a farm in the country you are coming from. If you are taking any form of medication, it is wise to have a doctor's letter as proof that you are not bringing in illicit substances. There is very little assistance for health problems in the USA, and treatment is very costly, so along with insurance for baggage, theft or trip-cancellation costs you should most definitely take out comprehensive medical insurance for the duration of your visit.

Getting There

By Air: The airports are within easy reach of the city. There are coach connections to **Grand Central** and the **Port Authority (PA)** from **Kennedy** and **LaGuardia**, to the PA from **Newark**. Morning and evening rush hours can lengthen the time taken considerably. There are car rental offices and usually numerous taxis on hand. There is now a fixed taxi fare from JFK to Manhattan – around $35 plus tolls and tip. There are few services between midnight and 06:00.

By Rail: The bargain from Kennedy to Midtown Manhattan is the subway which is less than an hour's duration and is a flat fare (about $2). The new AirTrain at Kennedy (about $5, www.panynj.com) takes you from terminals for transfers then to Howard Beach–JFK Station, or car parking, or Long Island trains at the Jamaica stop. The fast subway A train goes to express stops on the Eighth Avenue line in Manhattan. Some hotels provide courtesy coaches, there is a Monorail connection to JFK, and the new Penn Station to Newark AP is in operation.

By Road: Drive on the right. Roads into Manhattan are major highways, and well marked. Cars pay tolls at most entry points. In the city, roads can be badly deformed and pot-holed: drive carefully. Traffic lights are synchronised along main avenues. Drivers need to carry their licenses and for self-drive cars, full insurance should definitely be considered.

What to Pack

Dress is generally informal, although if you plan to play high stakes and live the smart life of Manhattan you will need fashionable wear, formal gear for

good restaurants, including jackets and ties for men and no jeans. Comfortable shoes are important, but they don't have to be unattractive, just well broken in. It can be very cold in winter, so pack warm clothes, take gloves and scarves, and you may need to get galoshes if it is snowing. This can be a place of extremes, and though New York streets are cleaned quickly, as a rule pavements can be very messy. Take a folding umbrella and rainwear. It is cool and temperate in the short spring and the longer fall, but it can get very hot and frightfully humid in summer when shorts, blouses or lightweight shirts are necessary. For summer cocktail parties or dinners, however, take lightweight formal wear.

Money Matters

The American dollar (a buck) is the unit and each dollar is divided into 100 cents. Coins are issued in denominations of 1c (called a cent or sometimes a penny), 5c (a nickel), 10c (a dime), 25c (a quarter), 50c and a dollar (dollar coins are not common except in some western states). Notes (paper money) are available in denominations of $1, $2 (rare), $5, $10, $20, $50, $100, $500 and up. Designs of notes are not too different and the basic colour is the same green, so check carefully when paying in cash. Paper money and coins have hardly changed at all except for metal content, which is a bonus as cash or coinage from previous trips will still be legal tender. The American dollar has fallen against many currencies over the past decade but has stabilized recently.

Currency Exchange: Most currencies are easily exchanged for dollars, and there are no restrictions except that you may not bring more than $10,000 in cash into the USA without making a declaration to Customs. You can take in cash below this limit, or dollar travellers' cheques, and you can exchange money at airport and station booths or at machines taking credit cards or some bank cards.

Banks: There are some national banks in the USA, and many private ones. Open 🕒 09:00–15:00 Mon–Fri. Cash machines taking most credit and bank cards are everywhere. Banks will need some form of identification for business other than exchanging cash, such as when changing travellers' cheques. Take a photo ID or a passport. Hotels will change money, but their rates won't necessarily be the best. Accredited dealers and travel agents have outlets in main centres, but it's wise to compare rates, especially

if cashing large amounts of money.

Credit Cards: The major ones (Visa, Access, American Express, Diners, Delta and Mastercard) are accepted everywhere for many transactions from shopping to gas (petrol). You can also use them to get cash. Practically all hotels, restaurants, travel agents and hire companies accept plastic. It is wise, however, to take out an insurance policy against theft on all your credit cards.

Tipping: Regardless of the quality of service (or lack of it), most people add 15% to restaurant and bar bills, taxi fares and services from hotel room staff. Beware the wrath of some drivers, porters or waiters untipped in certain restaurants. Porters often have a fixed rate. When checking out remember there will be City and State taxes added to your bill (also on shopping and meals).

Gambling: You can gamble in many ways in New York. Popular are horse racing, results of boxing or wrestling matches and other sports.

Accommodation

A vast range of prices, from the most luxurious hotels in the world to simple motels on the West Side or even bed-and-breakfasts. And for students and the budget-minded there are plain down-to-earth dormitory hostels.You can book ahead using services or there are booking facilities for hotels at airports and stations.

Eating Out

You are spoiled for choice in New York, with every kind of food from the best of Parisian-style and New York cooking to soul food. Many snack bars offer sandwiches; some favourites such as pastrami, salt beef and, of course, big hamburgers are bargains. Pretzels and

Maps and Farecards

The **Metropolitan Transportation Authority (MTA)** produces maps of New York's subway and bus routes. A free copy of the subway map is available at any subway station booth. The MTA maps used in this guide are current as of June 2005 and are subject to change.

MetroCard®, a magnetic farecard, is the primary fare media for the New York subway and bus systems. MetroCard may be purchased at many locations and used at all subway stations and on all public and many private buses within New York City. If you use a MetroCard, you can transfer free of charge between subway and bus, bus and subway and bus to bus. One-, seven- and thirty-day unlimited ride MetroCards are available. MetroCard vending machines, which accept cash, credit and debit cards, are located at many subway stations.

MTA Passenger Information

☎ 718 330 1234 (for people who speak English), and

☎ 718 330 4847 (for people who do not speak English)

Good Reading
While you are in New York City, don't forget to get hold of a copy of *The New York Times* or *Village Voice* for news and information on current events. There are also several magazines, such as *The New Yorker*, the *New York Magazine* and *Time Out Magazine*, which are very interesting and filled with helpful information.
- **Morrone, Francis**, *The Architectural Guidebook to New York City* (Gibbs-Smith).
- **Alleman, Richard**, *The Movie Lover's Guide to New York* (Harper & Row).

Useful Words
elevator • lift
sidewalk • pavement
subway • underground, metro
neat • good
apartment • flat
corn • maize
candy • sweets
nosh • eat
stores • shops
dim sum • Chinese dumplings
gumbo • stew
nickel • 5 cents
dime • 10 cents
quarter • 25 cents
buck • dollar

bagels are typical snacks. Steak houses offer grilled meats and salads at competitive prices. Local restaurants have special offers, big sandwiches and desserts.

Transport

New York has a well-developed, reasonable public transport system. The subway runs 24 hours a day and is extensive, covering four boroughs; it operates on a flat fare system. There's also the Staten Island Railway, not part of the subway system. Bus services on main avenues and cross streets at flat fare, sometimes transfers to and from subways are possible. New York is a terminus for many airlines and trains. Coaches and trains provide airport connections to Grand Central Terminal and the Port Authority.

Women Travellers: There are many precautions that need to be considered in a city like New York where a solitary woman can feel unsafe in some areas. Though less of a problem over the past decade, it's important to appear confident and alert, and you can be better prepared by going to information offices and asking about safety in the city.

Business Hours

Americans seem to work longer and longer hours, and New York is no exception with the bizarre 'power breakfasts' starting as early as ⌚ 06:30. Business, however, doesn't get geared up at most offices until 08:30 or 09:00 and goes on, often without lunch breaks, to 17:30 or 18:00, Mon–Fri. Banks are open ⌚ 09:00–15:00, but many have 24-hour automatic cash machines (you may need to swipe a bank or credit card to enter the space). Shops and supermarkets stay open later

on most evenings (Thursday shopping to ⌚ 21:00 at department stores) and are also open on Sundays. Some food stores serve customers past midnight. Fruit, veg and food stalls, especially along the lower East Side avenues, are open all night as are some cafés and snack bars, which even if they are not 24-hour operations, start early and close late. Many bars, of which there is a great variety in New York, are open all day and often only close for a couple of hours at night, usually from 04:00–06:00 to clean up. Big hotels will have round the clock reception and room service facilities.

Time Difference

New York is five hours behind GMT, and puts its clocks forward one hour in summer.

Communications

Telecommunications: Public telephones in the city are run by several companies. Numbers consist of a three-digit code and seven-digit numbers. Manhattan numbers are prefixed either 212 or 646 – even local calls must be prefixed with their three-digit code. For all calls beyond Manhattan you need to add 1 before the ten digits. The 800 calls are toll-free numbers, 900 numbers are definitely not, and they can be costly. Directory assistance for local calls is ☎ 411, for long distance dial ☎ 555 1212 prefixing with the usual 1 and the area code. Make person-to-person or collect calls or pay with coins, using public phones, but as this can mean a large handful of loose change for calls made through the operator from public phones it's best to buy a telephone card, or to use any one of several credit cards.

Help Lines: There are a number of help telephone lines to assist you. The Yellow Pages list agencies and counselling aids.

Postal services: Post offices are based at each zip code area of the city, with the main one at ✉ 34th Street and 8th Avenue being New York 10001. (The whole country has five-digit codes, and to speed delivery sometimes there is an additional four digit number attached). Postage varies from postcards to local mail and if you need special stamps there is sometimes a particular counter. All services, plus copying and faxing, are offered in most offices. If you need to receive mail, tell correspondents to send letters, allowing plenty of delivery time, ✉ c/o General Delivery at New York City, NY addressed to the specific zip code of the office at which you wish to pick up mail. Post offices are open ⌚ 08:00–17:00 Mon–Fri and 08:00–

12:00 Sat. Closed on all public holidays.

Electricity

The system uses 110-120 volts 60 cycles. The plugs are two-pin, so ensure converters will work in the USA.

Weights and Measures

The USA refuses to go metric, unlike Canada, and abides by the old imperial system. They use the regular gallon (not the imperial) and pints for liquids. They have little idea of metric equivalents so if buying shoes or clothes you may need to convert. Temperatures are measured in **Fahrenheit**.

Health Precautions

Do not even think of going to New York without taking out medical insurance. Buy it for the trip, as part of a regular insurance policy, or at the last minute where it can be purchased at some airports. It could cost a fortune to fall ill here without coverage, for though hospitals are right up to date they are very costly. There are some free hospitals ('charity' ones) but they are crowded, overworked and often understaffed; otherwise all hospitals are private. You can see a general practitioner or in an emergency go to a casualty ward. They usually want proof that you can pay your bill before offering services (often a recognized credit card imprint suffices). However, they **must** treat you regardless of this pressure.

Health Services

These are very minimal unless you are prepared to pay substantially. New York has the best hospitals and clinics, but you'll need a credit card. It's imperative to take out health insurance for a visit here. Note NYTAB offers a UK or Euro policy.

Personal Safety

It's sensible not to look like a tourist. Try and avoid obvious clothes and appendages such as camera bags. And most importantly for women, conceal or don't wear jewellery. Keep your wallet or purse in one pocket and have ready money in another, or wear a money belt under your clothing. Take only what you need, maybe concealing an extra note somewhere about your person, although muggers have been known to check inside shoes. Carry at least one, preferably two, forms of identification. On the streets, walk as if you know where you are going; dawdling and too much 'rubber-necking' can mark you out. Avoid poor and dangerous areas, and at night don't walk in parks. Don't get caught up with con artists – there are lots of them in the

city, operating all sorts of tricks. Hustlers are common in certain areas such as the Pennsylvania Station. Ask directions from policemen or doormen or BIDs, or go into shops or cafés. Never leave anything that looks valuable and that can be seen in a car. If you are travelling at night it's preferable to use surface transport but if there is no bus, then stay near subway token booths until the train arrives. Late at night the safest form of transport is a taxi.

Senior Citizens: If you are taking medication, or may need assistance, remember to keep a note to that effect on your person in order to pass on the information to a helper.

Emergencies

Embassies and Consulates: New York has a large representation of consulates, listed in the telephone book. If you require assistance from your embassy, you may need to contact the capital, Washington. There are UN missions from most countries based in New York.

Language

English is spoken everywhere in the USA, but in some neighbourhoods you will still hear a European tongue or even Yiddish. Almost everyone understands and speaks English, but in some cities, notably New York and Miami, **Spanish** is very much a major second language. The influx of Mexicans has made Spanish a second language in LA, but it is mostly due to the Puerto Rican influx in NYC that many hardly use English at all. The arrival of new Caribbean and South American settlers has brought French and Portuguese into the mix. You might have a French-speaking Haitian as a cab driver!

Useful Contacts

Big Apple Greeters: volunteers who offer an insider's point of view of New York, ☎ 212 669 2896.

Entertainment Information: a free service updated daily to inform you what's on in New York, 24-hour service, ☎ 360 3333.

New York City Onstage: for all arts events, 24 hours, ☎ 212 768 1818.

Theater Tkts: a booth selling half-price theatre tickets, ⊠ Times Square, ⊠ Front and John streets, ⊠ South Street Seaport. Queue for day of performance tickets for events on and off Broadway.

Post Office: the main one is at ⊠ Eighth Avenue and 33rd Street.

Tourist offices: ⊠ Lobby of Embassy Theater, 47th and Broadway; ⊠ Bloomingdale's, Third Avenue; ⊠ Macy's, 34th Street; ⊠ Grand Central Terminal; ⊠ Kennedy Airport. ⊕ 09:00–17:00 daily.

NYTAB: To pick up a free map, guide, or discount coupon book, call ☎ 212 267 1922.

Time: to find out the time, call ☎ 212 976 1616.

Weather: information on television or in newspapers or call ☎ 212 976 1212.

Index of Sights

Page numbers given in **bold** type indicate photographs